ROOM FOR Romance

THE ULTIMATE GUIDE TO ROMANTIC HOTELS

UK AND IRELAND

SECOND EDITION

FOREWORD

There are hotels and there are hotels. And finding just the right one for a blissful romantic encounter can be arduously hard work.

So relax. This revised, redesigned and much expanded second UK & Ireland edition of Room for Romance should make your quest as easy as falling into bed.

The 140 hotels, inns and country houses featured within these pages are tailor-made for romance, whether you're after a remote Highland hideaway, a blue-blooded English manor house or a charismatic inn on the wild shores of Wales or Ireland. No matter if your taste is trad or hip, urban or in-the-sticks, classic country or rustic chic, we think you'll find the place you're looking for here.

Needless to say, if your idea of a hotel is simply somewhere to kip at the end of the day, this guide is not for you. It's easy enough to find bargain beds and perfunctory places, and you won't need help from us.

Room for Romance hotels are another breed. Some are destinations in their own right, offering shameless sybarites once unheard-of levels of comfort and indulgence. Others are simple but stylish properties run with flair and élan. But all share those essential qualities that make them tailor-made for a getaway à deux: they are rich in ambience and individuality, big on style, and passionate about great hospitality. Whether they boast seductive suites, stunning decor, a terrific setting or dining to die for, these are the places perfect for romantic adventures.

Scotland, England, Wales and Ireland have some of the world's most fabulously romantic places to stay, and we have enjoyed making the final selection of properties showcased here. We hope you'll love them as much as we do.

MAIRIONA COTTER

SERIES EDITOR	Mairiona Cotter
EDITOR	Mike North
DESIGN & PRODUCTION	Claire Peters
ILLUSTRATIONS	Christine Coirault/frogillo.com
MAPS	Jenny White
COVER RETOUCHING	Joe Buckley
WEBSITE CO-ORDINATOR	Chris Shipton
CONTRIBUTORS	Laurence Phillips, Sophie Mackenzie
	Liz Kavanagh, Melissa Shales
HOTEL CONSULTANTS	Michael Yeo, Maurice Moliver
RESEARCH	Ben Etherton
ADMIN	Linzi Alberto, Frieda Yeo
PUBLISHER	Mairiona Cotter
PRINTING	Artes Gráficas Toledo
DISTRIBUTION	Portfolio Books, +44 (0)20 8997 9000

Published in 2005
Freeway Media Ltd, 4 Ravey Street, London EC2A 4XX
T +44 (0)20 7739 1434   **F** +44 (0)20 7739 1424
info@room4romance.com   www.room4romance.com
info@freewaymedia.com   www.freewaymedia.com

ISBN 09-531746-7-0
Copyright © 2005 Freeway Media Ltd

UK & IRELAND BY REGION

- SCOTLAND
- NORTH
- MIDSHIRES
- COTSWOLDS
- EAST ANGLIA
- SOUTH
- LONDON
- WEST COUNTRY & CHANNEL ISLANDS
- WALES
- IRELAND

Inverness
Aberdeen
Oban
Glasgow
Edinburgh
Belfast
Newcastle-upon-Tyne
Windermere
York
Galway
Dublin
Manchester
Limerick
Chester
Nottingham
Killarney
Cork
Birmingham
Norwich
Aberystwyth
Stratford-upon-Avon
Cambridge
Pembroke
Swansea
Gloucester
Oxford
Cardiff
Bath
Plymouth
Exeter
Brighton
Dover
Isles of Scilly
Channel Islands

CONTENTS

You'll find this guide easy to use. Practical information is followed by the hotel listings, arranged by region. At the end there's a detailed round-up of What's On around the country – giving you plenty of reasons to pack up and go – indexes to help you find the place that's right for you, and details of special extras offered at many Room for Romance properties.

CHAMPAGNE
PERRIER JOUËT

Unforgettable.

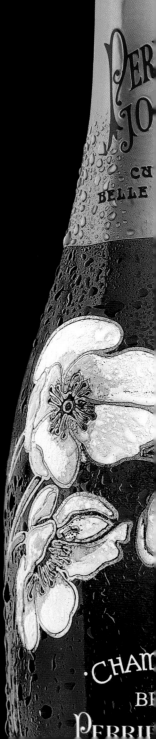

ABOUT ROOM FOR ROMANCE

Tailor-made for lovers of good hotels, Room for Romance guides are packed with details of places to fall in love with – and in love in. Turn these pages, and you'll find details of properties with all the essentials for a great romantic getaway – four-poster and canopied beds, roll-top baths, jacuzzis built for two, individually themed bedrooms and lots more. More editions are in the pipeline (read about our France edition on page 187), and our website at www.room4romance.com will keep you updated.

HOTELS OF THE YEAR

We invite readers to tell us which Room for Romance properties they feel are extra special. Our yearly hotel awards are announced each February, and the winners to date are listed here.

To tell us about a hotel you feel is a worthy Room for Romance award winner, we need to know your name and address, details of your visit and why you think the property in question is extra special.

You can contact us via our website or by emailing us at info@room4romance.com

HOTEL OF THE YEAR 2004
Amberley Castle
Nr. Arundel, Sussex

RUNNER-UP
Knockinaam Lodge
Portpatrick, Dumfries & Galloway

HOTEL OF THE YEAR 2003
Holbeck Ghyll
Windermere, Cumbria

RUNNER-UP
Combe House Hotel & Restaurant
Gittisham, Devon

SPECIAL ACCOLADES
The Witchery
Edinburgh
(Sexiest Suites)

Isle of Eriska
By Oban, Argyll
(Island Idyll)

Nonsuch House
Kingswear, Devon
(Chic on a Shoestring)

PRACTICALITIES

WHAT MAKES A ROOM FOR ROMANCE?

Everyone has a different take on just what makes a brilliantly romantic place to stay. It could be the setting, the style, the food or simply the blissful four-poster beds. Or perhaps an intangible quality that somehow makes it feel just right.

That's why the 140 properties we have included here are all different in terms of style, location and price. You'll find places here for every taste and occasion – whether it's thatched roofs and clambering roses in a rural time-warp, an extravagant big-city treat or all the grandeur of a medieval castle.

Forget the stars and facilities that preoccupy other guides – our aim has been to seek out the castles, manors, inns and townhouses whose feel and philosophy, location and loveliness make them tailor-made for romance. Almost all are privately owned, and run by people with a passion for high standards and service.

These are not places where you will be met with scripted corporate greetings, hordes of children (though some are of course child-friendly) or conference delegates. And whether village inn or five-star pleasure palace, they are among the best of their type.

Our choices are nonetheless subjective. We hope – though of course we cannot guarantee – that you will share our views. And we recognise that things can often change over time. Owners retire, chefs move on and properties that positively glow when they first open can lose their edge. We value your feedback (you can email us at info@room4romance.com) and our team will be pleased to follow up your comments.

SO WHAT'S NEW?

Hotel trends have moved on apace since publication of our first UK & Ireland edition. Country house hotels are no longer synonymous with floral decor and wall-to-wall chintz. Rustic chic, with its strong yet muted colours and clutter-free decor, is now much in vogue.

Bathrooms are now hedonistic havens on

a par with the bedroom, while spas bursting with body-pampering treatments for today's stressed workaholics are everywhere. Cutting-edge techno wizardry – whether plasma TVs set in the bathroom wall or Wifi (wireless internet) connections – are spreading fast. The hotels here naturally reflect these changing trends.

EATING AND DRINKING
Whether guests dine in a simple blackboard-menu bistro or a stunning Michelin star restaurant, Room for Romance properties are made for foodies. Many have award-winning chefs and kitchens, and an enthusiastic local following. Menus are becoming ever more eclectic, with the emphasis firmly on imaginatively used, locally sourced and seasonal ingredients.

Some properties here do not serve dinner, but you can expect an excellent breakfast, and plenty of advice on where to eat out. At others you'll enjoy sociable dinner-party style dining, giving you the chance to meet your fellow guests (and, perhaps, all the more excuse to slip off upstairs).

TARIFFS AND OTHER CHARGES
 The tariffs quoted on each page show the price range at a given property: that is, the entry cost of a standard double room for two, and that of the best room or suite available. Unless otherwise stated, rates are normally inclusive of full breakfast and VAT. Some rates include dinner and this generally represents excellent value for money.

While tariffs and other charges are correct at the time of going to press, they can of course change at short notice and should be treated as a guide, not a guarantee. High and low season rates will vary, and weekend surcharges may apply. Try and book well ahead, and do ask about special deals and discounts. If you're flexible on dates and days of the week, there are often bargains to be had.

Note that some hotels only accept two-night bookings at weekends. Almost all will require a credit card guarantee, and individual booking and cancellation terms may vary. Credit card surcharges may also apply.

Parking charges may be payable in city locations – especially in London, where street parking is at a premium and weekday congestion charges apply. It's worth checking on the details if you plan to arrive by car.

Most establishments will ask where you heard about them, and we appreciate you mentioning Room for Romance. It helps us ensure that our readers get the best in service and standards – as well as entitling you to the complimentary extras listed on pages 182-3.

R·R

ROOM FOR ROMANCE EXTRAS

Look out for the special R·R symbol on our hotel pages. This denotes properties where you will be welcomed by special – and often exclusive – extras such as a bottle of complimentary champagne, an upgraded room, a special gift or a West Country cream tea.

It's important that you identify yourself as a Room for Romance reader when booking to take advantage of these many great offers. Even if your chosen hotel does not list any specific extras, make sure the owners know you found them here. It help us ensure our readers get well taken care of in the future.

For full details of the extras on offer at individual Room for Romance hotels, turn to pages 182-3.

KEY TO SYMBOLS

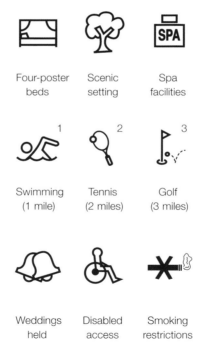

Four-poster beds	Scenic setting	Spa facilities
Swimming (1 mile)	Tennis (2 miles)	Golf (3 miles)
Weddings held	Disabled access	Smoking restrictions

These symbols denote some of the special features at each property.

OUR PAGE ENTRIES

Where possible, our writers point you towards the best, or most romantic, rooms and suites at each property. We also give an indication (albeit sometimes tongue in cheek) of the kind of people who stay at each place – whether it's A-list celebs, media types, the country set or food-loving bon vivants. We also sum up in a sentence what we think you'll love most about a particular place, or what makes it special. The contact name shown is generally the proprietor, but is otherwise the general manger.

SYMBOLS

The symbols shown alongside each entry denote facilities either at the hotel or nearby. We recommend that you check the details when booking if a particular item is of special interest.

Where amenities are not on site – golfing or tennis, for instance – the approximate distance in miles is shown alongside where known. The swimming symbol denotes a pool (whether indoor or outdoor), and/or occasionally nearby beach swimming. The disabled-friendly

symbol should denote wheelchair access to at least one bedroom as well as a hotel's public areas, while the smoking restrictions sign can mean a ban in both bedrooms and dining or bar areas. If you loathe (or like) smoking, it clearly pays to check details when booking. Finally, be aware that the hotel closure dates shown may vary somewhat from year to year.

SPAS

No two hotel spas are the same, so if you're after the ultimate body-pampering experience do check just what is on offer when you see our spa symbol. While spas in more expensive properties offer an impressive menu of treatments as well as all the trimmings, those in smaller hotels are more likely to comprise a sauna, jacuzzi and/or fitness room, and perhaps an on-call beauty therapist. We suggest you check when booking rather than risk disappointment.

www.room4romance.com

Do visit www.room4romance.com. You can find out about other editions of Room for Romance, check out special short breaks available at different times of the year and order further copies of this guide online. You can see what the press says about us, and click through to the websites of every property featured here. You can also email us your views and feedback, as well as registering your vote for our Hotel of the Year awards.

YOUR KIND OF PLACE

Know the kind of place you're after but not sure how to find it? Then turn to pages 184-5, where properties have been loosely grouped by type to make the job easier. Thus if only a real castle will do, or you have to have a spa on site, you can easily find the properties that match your needs. Those listed under the "food comes first" banner are mainly restaurants with rooms, gastro-inns and hotels with serious culinary accolades.

SPECIAL THANKS

Many people have helped to bring this edition together, and it's impossible to acknowledge every one. Special thanks must go to Michael Yeo, our UK hotel consultant, and our hard-working in-house team, especially design and production editor Claire Peters.

SCOTLAND

Go for lochs, legends and Highland games
Eat haggis, neeps and tatties
Take a hip flask – you'll be wanting a wee dram
Bedtime story? Robbie Burns: *A Red, Red Rose*

John o'Groats

Scourie

Stornoway
Isle of Lewis

Ullapool
Dornoch
A816
27

North Uist
26
Elgin
29
Peterhead
25
Isle of Skye
Inverness
South Uist
Kyle of Lochalsh
28
Aberdeen
24 23
Rhum
Mallaig
30

Coll
Fort William
31
Tiree
22
20
Mull
21 Kyle of Lochalsh
Perth Dundee
19
32 St Andrews
Oban
18
34
33
M9 35
Stirling
Islay
A83
A82
41 38
Glasgow
Edinburgh
36 39 37
17
M74 40
Arran
Ayr
Campbeltown
A77
Stranraer
Dumfries
16
A75
30

Pages 16- 41

Knockinaam Lodge

Portpatrick
Dumfries & Galloway DG9 9AD
T 01776 810471
F 01776 810435
E reservations@knockinaamlodge.com
W www.knockinaamlodge.com
David & Sian Ibbotson

9 rooms
£200 to £370 per room per night
Dinner from £45

Open all year

From the A75/A77: head towards
Portpatrick. Two miles past Lochans,
turn left at the Smokehouse
and follow signs.

Lawns that slope down to a rugged beach bordering the Irish Sea, miles of cliff-top paths begging to be explored, deserted wooded hills and glens... the Famous Five would have loved it here, and so will you. Knockinaam is a ravishing retreat for lovers in search of peace and seclusion – a place to hide out, bunker down, snuggle up and let the scenic surroundings and attentive service dissolve away your cares. Exquisitely decorated bedrooms, bathrooms designed for preening, Michelin star cuisine and an awesome selection of malt whiskies and champagnes are just some of the things to write home about. But it's the feeling of seclusion that makes Knockinaam so special – it's hard to believe that you're just a couple of hours away from two major cities in this gorgeous corner of south-west Scotland. Not surprisingly, many of Knockinaam's guests think it's a knockout.

Love time   Churchill has a king-size sleigh bed and a 100-year-old bathtub for serious soaking; Bay has a Victorian half-tester and heart-stopping sea views.

Love bites   The dining room deserves every word of the praise that's been lavished on it. Your tastebuds are in for a treat from a daily-changing menu matched by an impressive cellar.

Love it up   Your hosts David and Sian will advise on walks, sightseeing, golf, riding and more – or you could just play a game of croquet on the lawn, soak up the scenery, and await your next meal!

Who loves?   Golfers, gourmets and the great and good – Winston Churchill was a fan.

You'll love   A foodie paradise miles from the beaten track.

SCOTLAND

One Devonshire Gardens

1 Devonshire Gardens
Glasgow G12 OUX
T 0141 339 2001
F 0141 337 1663
E reservations@onedevonshiregardens.com
W www.onedevonshiregardens.com
Stephen McCorkell

32 rooms, 3 suites
£150 to £495 per room per night
Dinner from £25

Open all year

From the M8 (J17): follow signs for the A82 to Dumbarton/Kelvinside along the Great Western Road. Travel for approx 1.5 miles and the hotel is at the junction with Hyndland Road.

RR

This stylish boutique hotel, made up of five Victorian townhouses in the heart of Glasgow's fashionable West End, is as elegant as they come. Self-assured in tone yet pleasingly understated, it's all cool creams and rich chocolate, low lighting and tasteful prints. Rooms are ultra-comfortable, and styled with a bold mix of the trad and contemporary. The property has just been refurbished at a grand cost of £2 million, and its new Room Glasgow restaurant is fast becoming *the* chic place to eat out. Head-turning colour combos – midnight blue, off-white and scarlet, for instance – make some bedrooms real head-turners, while others play on creams and neutrals. Full-length drapes, extravagant ties and tassels, chaises longues, elegant lamps and sleek bathrooms full of shining chrome and dark wood underline the sense of expansive comfort. The hotel has been wowing the critics for some time, winning a place in *Conde Nast Traveller's* 2004 Gold List. You'll soon see why.

Love time   Room 29's palatial bathroom comes complete with a party shower made for fun and frolics.

Love bites   Go retro in Room Glasgow, where classics like prawn cocktail, lamb goulash and jelly and ice cream are given an ultra-contemporary twist. Alternatively go grown-up in No. 5, known for its fine Scottish cuisine.

Love it up   Hit the Charles Rennie Mackintosh trail for a taste of Art Nouveau Glasgow, or let yourself loose in Scotland's best stores.

Who loves?   A roll-call of celebs includes Kylie, Robbie Williams and Ewan McGregor.

You'll love 🖋   Sleek surroundings with star quality.

Ardanaiseig

Kilchrenan, by Taynuilt
Argyll PA35 1HE
T 01866 833333
F 01866 833222
E info@ardanaiseig.com
W www.ardanaiseig.com
Peter Webster

16 rooms, 1 cottage
£45 to £145 per person per night
Dinner from £42

Closed early Jan – mid Feb

From Glasgow or Oban: take the A85 to the B845 (one mile east of Taynuilt). Continue to Kilchrenan, turning left at the inn onto the single track road leading to Ardanaiseig.

RR

Myth has it that Ardanaiseig was built on ancient settlements by those drawn here by the magic well of youth whose crystal waters formed Loch Awe on Scotland's west coast. You can still feel the spell; it's a wildly romantic setting at the end of a winding road, and one where this imposing baronial mansion commands enviable views of the loch, crannogs and little islands (one of which is their own) amid 100 acres of woodlands littered with exotic plants. You'll want to cut a swathe through the interior; we loved the bold midnight blue walls and stippled gold paintwork setting off chunky Gothic furniture and owner Bennie Gray's remarkable paintings. Reception areas are decorated with choice chintz, while a log fire sizzles in the grate. Bedrooms feel effortlessly arty, and all have loch or garden views. The dining room looks out over water, and the only distraction (apart from your partner) will be chef Gary Goldie's well composed cuisine. Lovers of Scotch can wallow over one of the fine cellared whiskies before dinner.

Love time   Soak in Cuaig's decadent gold bath, or drop anchor in the ultra-private Boat House suite (from Easter '05), right on the water's edge.

Love bites   Seafood is a speciality, caught that day; the menu tempts with pan-fried sea bass or seared scallops, for example. Just-picked herbs from the garden add perky notes to dishes. Try one, two or three of some 50 malts.

Love it up   Go mountain hiking (you're in reach of 12 Munros) or take a picnic to the hotel's own private island in the loch.

Who loves?   Couples who love it on the wild side.

You'll love   It's ruggedly romantic outside; moodily romantic within.

The Airds Hotel & Restaurant

Port Appin, Appin
Argyll PA38 4DF
T 01631 730236
F 01631 730535
E airds@airds-hotel.com
W www.airds-hotel.com
Shaun & Jenny McKivragan

11 rooms, 1 suite
£230 to £360 per room per night
Dinner from £45

Closed 5-26 Jan

From Glasgow: take the M8 West, join
the A82 (Crianlarich) and head North to
Ballachulish. Take the A828 to Oban and
in Appin turn right at the sign for
Port Appin/Lismore Ferry.

Its location in attractive Port Appin in the West Highlands with great views of Loch Linnhe makes The Airds a great base on Scotland's west coast. This is where you fall under the spell of mountains soaring from water to sky, where light is luminescent, and the peace is almost palpable (yes, it does feel that poetic!). The hotel continues such lightness of heart. Built during the 18th century as a ferry inn, its warm, hospitable vibe pervades the two comfy reception rooms with flowers, books and log fires. The little conservatory is just the place for clocking that gorgeous scenery, while nicely done-up bedrooms in country-house colours deliver on all fronts, too. Guests come not least for the cooking of J Paul Burns, Scottish Hotel Chef of the Year 2004. Meals might include Aberdeen Angus beef, fillet of turbot or lasagne of wild mushrooms with asparagus and pesto. Desserts are toothsome, and the presentation is slick. Owners Shaun and Jenny McKivragan and their staff sprinkle service with stardust.

Love time The Superior suite has a state-of-the-art music system, bedside whisky decanter, and wide-open views.

Love bites The chef's award-winning cooking is right up there; expect great fish, beef, game and true veggie delights.

Love it up Order a picnic hamper and a bottle of champagne and take scenic walks or boat trips; go island-hopping (Lismore, Mull, Iona); shoot, fish and ride, or simply laze by the fireside.

Who loves? Stella McCartney stays; not to mention gourmets, painters and hill walkers.

You'll love ▸ Being cosseted like a laird at Airds.

Isle of Eriska

Ledaig, by Oban
Argyll PA37 1SD
T 01631 720371
F 01631 720531
E office@eriska-hotel.co.uk
W www.eriska-hotel.co.uk
The Buchanan-Smith family

22 rooms
£260 to £360 per room per night
Dinner from £38.50

Closed January

From Glasgow: Take the A82 North, then follow the A85 towards Oban. At Connel proceed by bridge to the village of Benderloch. Eriska is well signposted from there.

This dreamy castellated house, set on its very own private island, is a storybook lovers' hideaway. Cross the causeway from the mainland and you enter a world of peace and tranquillity where highland cattle graze, badgers nest, and grey seals frolic in the waters. Indoors, you'll be welcomed by friendly staff for whom nothing is too much trouble. The Buchanan-Smith family have spent 30 years perfecting every detail of this very special hotel, and it just keeps getting better. Top-quality fresh produce is sourced locally and prepared with consummate skill by head chef Robert MacPherson. The Veranda restaurant at the Stables spa is perfect for a post-treatment lunch that will leave you feeling virtuously healthy. Recent additions include ultra-private cottage and spa suites, and a conservatory restaurant where you can admire the scenery while you dine. There's a small but perfectly formed six-hole golf course, a spa complete with sauna, pool, steam room and treatment rooms, and woods to wander through. Best of all, this sumptuous island haven is just two hours' drive from Glasgow and Edinburgh.

Love time   Eriska's brand new spa suites boast wickedly private open-air hot tubs. Keep it clean, please.

Love bites   Scotch beef here is a must, as are wild mushrooms and salmon fresh from the loch. Veggies and herbs are home-grown and zing with flavour.

Love it up   Explore the island's 300 acres on foot, pamper yourselves in the luxurious spa, or have a pop at a few clay pigeons.

Who loves?   Savvy sybarites who come here year after year.

You'll love ♥ Watching the sunset over the Western Isles – a true champagne moment.

Hebridean Princess

Griffin House, Broughton Hall, Skipton
North Yorkshire BD23 3AN
T 01756 704704
F 01756 704794
E reservations@hebridean.co.uk
W www.hebridean.co.uk

30 cabins
Double cabin for 2 people
per 7 night cruise, including meals
from £1490 per person

Operates March – November

The ship's specially chartered coach will meet you at Glasgow Airport or rail station and take you to the Argyll port of Oban for embarkation.

Romancing on the high seas has to be the ultimate high – especially amid the incomparable splendour of the Western Isles. This cachet-laden cruiser – all sumptuous comfort, teak decks and polished brass – lets you explore the rugged shores of Scotland and Ireland in the enviable style of a floating country house. Motor launches whisk you ashore to visit dramatic lochs, ruined castles and untrodden islands in this scenic corner of Europe – a wildlife haven teeming with seabirds and seals – where you can pedal off on the ship's bicycles, amble through pretty seaports or turn wildlife photographer. Back on board, dress for cocktails or a sterling black tie dinner before sleeping to the soporific sound of waves lapping against the hull as the ship drops anchor in some secluded bay. Guests get the royal treatment from the word go, feasting on superb fare and shamelessly spoilt by an attentive crew whose sole aim is to please. While this floating nirvana doesn't come cheap, it doesn't come finer.

Love time	Beautifully fitted out cabins are matched by marble bathrooms complete with robes and the fluffiest towels.
Love bites	Breakfasts are legendary, while dinners are prepared by some of Scotland's most talented young chefs. Drool over fresh-landed oysters, pot-roasted quail or pan-seared skate wing.
Love it up	Glimpse untamed horizons ashore, then watch the sun sink over the Western Isles with a wee dram on deck.
Who loves?	Nautically inclined princes and princesses.
You'll love	Lapping up the luxury of it all.

Highland Cottage

Breadalbane Street, Tobermory,
Isle of Mull, Argyll PA75 6PD
T 01688 302030
F 01688 302727
E davidandjo@highlandcottage.co.uk
W www.highlandcottage.co.uk
David & Jo Currie

6 rooms
£120 to £150 per room per night
Dinner from £35

Closed end Oct – end Feb (ex. New Year)

From the ferry: follow the road to
Tobermory. At the mini roundabout
cross the narrow bridge and go
immediately right into Breadalbane
Street. Continue along this road.
The hotel is opposite the Fire Station.

More of a spruce seaside villa than a cottage, this place is nonetheless a wee gem.
Taking the ferry from Oban across to Mull makes a visit here appealingly escapist, and
the house is set just a short distance from the distinctive row of brightly painted seafront
houses of the island capital Tobermory. Owners Jo and David Currie run Highland
Cottage with zeal and dedication. There are books to curl up with in the upstairs
lounge, an old dresser stacked with malts, lamp-lit rooms, a sunny conservatory and
vases of fresh flowers. In keeping with the property's cottagey name, bedrooms (all
island-themed) are cosy and snug, with pretty four-posters and pastel decor. Cooking
here is affordable, unpretentious and top-notch (it's rated the best restaurant on Mull),
so expect well-hung Highland beef and Atlantic-fresh seafood among Jo's award-
winning repertoire of dishes. Outside the door, Mull's rugged hills and cliffy coves await
exploration. This is the place to walk, go bird watching or simply watch the action in the
busy little harbour, where seals can often be spotted. A homely welcome awaits within
after the exhilaration of the great outdoors.

Love time   Book Staffa or Nantucket, with their lovely carved four-poster beds.
Love bites   Dinner here is a hot ticket among locals and visitors alike. "Jo cooks like
                 an angel," noted one recent reviewer. We think you'll agree.
Love it up   Visit the ancient standing stones at Baliscate, take a boat trip out to Staffa
                 or walk a woodland trail in nearby Aros Park.
Who loves?   Island aficionados in search of a home from home.

You'll love Delectable fare, divine scenery.

Glenelg Inn

Glenelg Bay, Ross-shire
IV40 8JR
T 01599 522273
F 01599 522283
E christophermain7@glenelg-inn.com
W www.glenelg-inn.com
Christopher Main

7 rooms
£100 to £160 per room per night
Dinner from £29

Open all year

From Inverness or Fort William: take the A887/A87 to Shiel Bridge, turn left onto the country road and follow signs to Glenelg Inn.

Not quite over the sea to Skye but facing it just across the water, Glenelg Inn is brilliantly located amid hills and glens on the water's edge, its gardens cascading right down to the shore. Its name is said to derive from the Gaelic "Gleann Seilg" (Glen of Hunting), and walls are not surprisingly hung with antlers. The sitting room has a warm home-from-home feel, with leather chesterfields and comfy sofas, family portraits on the walls and assorted knick-knacks. Locals and visitors happily mingle in the oak-beamed bar, where live pipe and fiddle music is a regular feature. Genial owner Christopher Main gives the place a nicely hospitable vibe, and is happy to suggest places nearby for wildlife-spotting, pony trekking, fishing and hill walking. Comfortable, uncluttered bedrooms are individually decorated and all offer unrestricted views of Skye. We're told there's an impressive record of conception here – apparently due to the ley (that's right) lines running through the village. Those not out to procreate swear by the recuperative powers of the soft, peaty bath water.

Love time   Room Seven is an ultra-private suite, while others score best on views.
Love bites   Expect good-value wholesome Scottish fare, with fish and seafood a speciality. We loved west coast red mullet with a sweet red pepper dressing on roasted greens.
Love it up   Explore the many lochs, tiny islands and hidden caves that inspired Gavin Maxwell's *Ring of Bright Water,* or see the seals and sea otters at Kylerhea.
Who loves?   Bill Bryson famously dubbed the Inn "an outpost of comfort and graciousness."
You'll love   Home-from-home charm and views you could bottle.

Eilean Iarmain

Sleat, Isle of Skye IV43 8QR
T 01471 833332
F 01471 833275
E hotel@eileaniarmain.co.uk
W www.eileaniarmain.co.uk
Archie MacCalman

12 rooms, 4 suites
£125 to £235 per room per night
Dinner from £31

Open all year

From Kyle of Lochalsh: cross the bridge to Skye and continue on the A87. Turn left onto the A851 for Sleat and Isle Ornsay. The hotel is ten minutes from the Mallaig-Armadale ferry.

Head Skyewards, and you'll find this little privately owned hotel on a sheltered bay with poetic views over the Sound of Sleat towards the Scottish mainland. You're in the heart of Gaelic country here: owner Sir Iain Noble has championed the language's rebirth and it's widely spoken here. Flora MacDonald was taken captive at the tiny harbour back in 1746, and the place still resonates with history. Inside, all is snug Highland charm and old-world atmosphere. Sink into an old-fashioned sofa by the log fire, and prepare for intimate candlelit dinners in the beamed dining room overlooking the bay. Country-cosy pine panelling and fireplaces, floral chintzes and warm pastel-painted walls characterise the bedrooms, all kitted with robes and a warming dram of local Te Bheag whisky. The 19th century stables have been converted into spacious split-level suites, prettily done out with toiles and checks and with terrific views across the water.

Love time Honeymooners love to disappear into Room Two, whose extra-generous, antique canopied bed once graced nearby Armadale Castle.

Love bites Chef Graham Smith makes the most of the estate's native game and home-reared lamb. Start with langoustines landed at the old stone pier and oysters fresh from the hotel's own oyster beds. Try a game terrine, or a medley of local seafood poached in saffron and Chablis.

Love it up Take a sea safari to clock colonies of seals and the towering Cuillins. Go walking, sailing, shooting (woodcock, snipe and pheasant) or even stalking.

Who loves? Then: poets and artists. Now: fans of the sporting life (and their comforts).

You'll love ❤ Gaelic overtones in a place worth coming over the sea to Skye for.

Three Chimneys

Colbost, Dunvegan
Isle of Skye IV55 8ZT
T 01470 511258
F 01470 511358
E eatandstay@threechimneys.co.uk
W www.threechimneys.co.uk
Eddie & Shirley Spear

6 junior suites
£215 per night
Dinner from £45

Closed three weeks Jan

From Portree: take the A87/A850 to Dunvegan. Then take the B884 to Glendale and travel five miles to Colbost.

Longstanding fans of this superb Skye restaurant were over the moon when its six luxury suites opened in 1999, enabling them to stay on for the night – or several. Owners Eddie and Shirley Spear are passionate about food (as you will be after dining here). The only Scottish address to be included in *Restaurant* Magazine's list of the world's 50 best restaurants, it has been rightly showered in culinary awards. Not that good food is the only attraction here. Skye's rugged north coast stretches away beyond the French windows, inviting hand-in-hand, windswept strolls along rocky beaches complete with basking seals, lochs and clifftops. What's more, every home comfort awaits your return. Sink into the velvety two-seater sofa, watch a film, listen to CDs and crack open a bottle of champers in your split-level suite. Then climb into your king-size bed, light a candle and gaze out at a starlit sky from between the sheets.

Love time   Heart-stoppingly gorgeous views come as standard in each of the six sumptuous suites.

Love bites   Menus are strictly seasonal, using the very best local produce and terrific fresh Skye seafood. Highland beef, lamb and game are superb (try the pan-fried breast of wood pigeon to start) while sweets are positively sinful. Finish your feast with hot marmalade pudding and Drambuie custard.

Love it up   Chill out, soak up the scenery and indulge yourselves in this peaceful island haven.

Who loves?   Foodies the world over: this is the place for a pilgrimage.

You'll love   Gourmet heaven where the Skye's the limit.

Flodigarry Country House

Staffin, Isle of Skye IV51 9HZ
T 01470 552203
F 01470 552301
E info@flodigarry.co.uk
W www.flodigarry.co.uk
Robert Cairns

18 rooms
£100 to £190 per room per night
Dinner from £30

Open all year

From Portree: take the A855 to Staffin,
and continue North for a few miles.

We're on the Isle of Skye's romantic north-east coast. Nestled below Quiraing Mountain, Flodigarry sits safely above the waves of Staffin Bay while promising pleasures in full flood. Quaint whitewashed Flora's Cottage is tucked into the secluded grounds beside this original 19th century fortress with its pretty garden. Here's where legendary Scottish heroine Flora MacDonald lived after helping Bonnie Prince Charlie flee Culloden's battlefield in 1746. The place is still an escape: perfection for wildlife lovers who, on coming indoors, get swept up in the hospitable embrace of warmly furnished rooms and crackling fires. Bedrooms are a delight, with antiques aplenty, tartans and wood and (in some) Victorian cast iron baths. Panoramic sea and mountain views abound. Top-notch cuisine calls on the island's freshest ingredients, with dinners beautifully served by candlelight. Seafood is caught daily, produce is garden-grown while breads are home-baked. Enjoy a dram of Talisker house malt or join in a foot-tapping ceilidh complete with pipe and fiddles. Owner Robert Cairns tends Flodigarry with panache.

Love time   Flora's Cottage makes an adorable hideout, while the Quiraing and Torridon rooms enjoy four-posters and outstanding views.
Love bites   Enjoy relaxed silver-service dining with golden-touch cuisine that's big on seafood, beef and game.
Love it up   Share whispers in the secret lovers' garden, take scenic walks, go whale or wildlife watching or set sail on a boat trip (and fish for your supper).
Who loves?   Modern-day Floras and their leading men.

You'll love 🍂   A coastal Skye high.

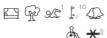

SCOTLAND

Pool House

Poolewe, by Achnasheen
Wester Ross IV22 2LD
T 01445 781272
F 01445 781403
E enquiries@poolhousehotel.com
W www.poolhousehotel.com
The Harrison family

5 suites
£265 to £395 per room per night
Dinner from £45

Closed early Jan – mid Feb

From Inverness Airport: head towards
Ullapool on the A835, then take
the A832 to Gairloch.

Tucked into the rugged mountains framing the shores of Loch Ewe, Pool House offers the best of both worlds. Overlooking the clear waters of the loch, this sumptuous hideaway practically rubs shoulders with the wildlife outside its doors, where local residents include seals, herons and otters. But even the distraction of nature in all its elements can't detract from the luxury that awaits inside. Awash with Victorian splendour, this one-time Scottish courthouse is a feast of antique portraits and porcelain, roaring fires and top-notch cuisine. All five suites (created from 14 original rooms) are atmospheric, with Victorian brass, French antiques, feature fireplaces, clawfoot baths and canopied beds. Rooms downstairs are equally full of charm – the cosy library is stacked with books, while the Billiard Whisky room is a cosy setting for a malt or two. Rooms are splashed with golden light at sunset and lucky guests may even spot a sea eagle or two or – in wintertime – the Aurora Borealis.

Love time	Go overboard in The Diadem suite (styled on the lines of the Titanic), with its 1912 bathtub and glass canopied shower. The only sinking you'll be doing is into the seven-foot square four-poster.
Love bites	Stargaze in the gilded dining room, with its hand-painted zodiac ceiling. Award-winning fare makes full use of locally-farmed meat and produce.
Love it up	Hike on rugged mountain trails or count the blooms in sub-tropical Inverewe Gardens.
Who loves?	Lovers out for a Highland fling.
You'll love	Rugged nature without, sumptuous style within.

RR

Minmore House

Glenlivet, Banffshire
AB37 9DB
T 01807 590378
F 01807 590472
E minmorehouse@ukonline.co.uk
W www.minmorehousehotel.com
Lynne & Victor Janssen

10 rooms
£90 to £160 per room per night
Dinner from £35

Closed February

From the A9: take the A95 at Aviemore. Turn right onto the B9008 at Grantown-on-Spey and Minmore is just north of Tomintoul.

This award-winning, sweet-as-pie Scottish hideaway could be just the place for a flirty weekend in the Highlands. Edged by miles of glens and forests and just a stone's throw from the famous distillery, it sits at the heart of the Glenlivet Crown Estate amid the sweeping Grampian hills. Minmore's friendly managers Lynne and Victor Janssen encourage a house-party atmosphere and you're sure to meet your fellow guests in the wood-panelled bar or around the crackling fire. Arriving guests are treated to a full-blown Highland tea, complete with Lynne's famous chocolate whisky cake and home-baked scones. Be sure to work up an appetite for the delicious four-course candlelit dinner later, though: cooking here is the big highlight. Spacious bedrooms are filled with homely touches, while bathrooms are stocked with hand-made geranium and cinnamon soaps. Gaze out at the views from your bed or snuggle under the feather duvets. Minmore is a TV-free zone, so you won't be watching telly!

Love time   Sink into the grand four-poster of the bay-windowed Glenlivet room.

Love bites   House specialities include Gressingham duck and grilled prawns glazed with a 14-herb butter sauce, not to mention a mean apple and tarragon soufflé. There's an excellent South African wine list.

Love it up   You're just minutes from the famous distillery, while Ballindalloch Castle is a must-see. This is terrific country for walking, fishing and golf.

Who loves?   Couples with couples: this is just the place for your own house party.

You'll love   Victor's soufflés. "What does it profit a man if he gains the whole world but never tastes one of these?" wrote one fan.

SCOTLAND

Boath House

Auldearn, Nairn
IV12 5TE
T 01667 454896
F 01667 455469
E wendy@boath-house.com
W www.boath-house.com
Don & Wendy Matheson

6 rooms
£170 to £220 per room per night
Dinner £45

Closed over Christmas

From Inverness: take the A96 to Nairn.
The hotel is signed on the left.

This Regency manor house near the Moray Firth is winning accolades so fast we feel compelled to share it. Standing in 20 acres, the Boath House was a wreck just a decade ago. Enter new owners Don and Wendy Matheson, in whose hands it has been reborn as the area's plum new address. Guests feel instantly at home here: there's no check-in desk, no dress codes and no room keys. Service is exemplary, and they'll even serve you a late-late breakfast till midday. The flagstoned hallway, with its eclectic mix of contemporary art, leads the way to sprawling rooms in vibrant shades of cerise, purple and mustard with some of the most decadent bathrooms – all with made-to-wallow-in clawfoot baths – north of the border. High-maintenance townies can book blissful Aveda beauty treatments in the spa downstairs. But it's chef Charlie Lockley's dazzling Franco-Scottish cooking that puts this place on the map. Candlelit dinners are a visual and gastronomic treat in what has been voted one of Scotland's top ten restaurants.

Love time Room Three, with its side-by side clawfoot baths, is decadence itself.
Love bites Gorgeous dishes on the daily changing five-course dinner menu might include dived scallops, fillet of sea bass on puy lentils with a caper berry dressing or haunch of venison on celeriac puree with spiced red cabbage.
Love it up Staying in? Book the double jacuzzi and sauna downstairs. Heading out? Nairn's beaches, and the Speyside whisky trail, are just down the road.
Who loves? "People who want great food, good wine and some ooh-la-la," say the owners. We wouldn't argue.

You'll love ► An A1 place for the Boath of you.

Darroch Learg

Braemar Road, Ballater
Aberdeenshire AB35 5UX
T 01339 755443
F 01339 755252
E info@darrochlearg.co.uk
W www.darrochlearg.co.uk
Nigel & Fiona Franks

17 rooms
£100 to £160 per room per night
Dinner from £38

Closed Christmas and
last three weeks Jan

From Aberdeen: Take the A93 to
Ballater and at village, continue up
Darroch Brae past the turreted
Oakhall mansion. The hotel is
on the right.

From its vantage point high above Ballater, you can soak up views across the Dee Valley from the windows of Darroch Learg (Gaelic for "a copse on a sunny slope"), and if perchance there aren't any rays, fear not; true Scots warmth led by owners Nigel and Fiona Franks is ever-present in this handsome turreted Victorian mansion. Elegant reception rooms with antiques, watercolours, flowers and fires enjoy a touch of the baronial, while comfy chairs and log fires cry out for companionable pre- and post-prandial drinks. Prize-winning cooking is another big draw, and chef David Mutter invites guests to choose between a fine three-course dinner and a seven-course taster. Pace yourself (after a wee dram of the national nectar) for roasted sea scallops and breast of guinea fowl, with a white chocolate mousse to round off. The wine list includes some 230 bins, with finer vintages remarkably well priced. Rooms all make the grade in terms of comfort and furnishings; some period, some modern. The Franks have spent 40 years polishing things here. You can't help feeling they have got it just right.

Love time Try the queen-sized four-poster, antiques and Dee Valley views of Invercauld – one of the spacious master rooms.

Love bites Be seduced by tortellini of langoustine, Aberdeen Angus fillet with tarragon sauce, and classic lemon tart in the lamp-lit conservatory restaurant.

Love it up Explore Royal Deeside country and climb Craigendarroch; follow whisky, castle and heritage trails; or go fishing, stalking, gliding and golfing.

Who loves? Highland lads and lasses.

You'll love Feeling royal by association (Balmoral's just up the road).

Castleton House

by Glamis, Angus
DD8 1SJ
T 01307 840340
F 01307 840506
E hotel@castletonglamis.co.uk
W www.castletonglamis.co.uk
David Webster & Verity Nicholson

6 rooms
£100 to £200 per room per night
Dinner from £25 à la carte
3 course table d'hôte from £35

Open all year

From Perth: take the A93/A94 for Glamis.
The hotel is on the left just a few miles
before the town.

Just a stone's throw from Glamis and its famous castle, Castleton House offers regal comforts and a welcome to match. Owners David Webster and Verity Nicholson have lavished TLC on this antique-strewn country house, and jazzed it up with flair and originality. Friendly (and refreshingly local) staff are imbued with the infectious enthusiasm of the owners, and the place exudes a sense of cosseted good living and bonhomie. Rooms are tasteful to a T, and done out in impeccable country house style. There's stylish decor, original art, jugs of fresh flowers and plenty of plump pillows. Thoughtful in-room extras include a flask of iced water, next day's weather forecast and – lest you're stumped for ideas – bedtime stories. Eclectic menus are sourced from the best home-grown produce, and guests dine in the strikingly done out conservatory or more traditional dining room. Lemon and Lime, two ginger Tamworth pigs ("they're as friendly as labradors," promises David) rootle around in the orchard. Romance clearly blossoms here: David and Verity were planning their big day as we went to press.

Love time   Try the Regency four-poster suite; very Beau Brummel.
Love bites   Talented chef Andrew Wilkie now has three AA rosettes under his belt. Dine on tenderest Scottish beef, west-coast salmon or Highland lamb.
Love it up   You're just a few miles from Glamis castle, home of the late Queen Mother, and Kirriemuir, home of *Peter Pan* author JM Barrie.
Who loves?   Quite a guest list. You think they're name-dropping?

You'll love ❥   Slinky, silk monogrammed bathrobes – just the thing for when you fancy slipping into something more comfortable.

The Peat Inn

by Cupar, Fife
KY15 5LH
T 01334 840206
F 01334 840530
E reception@thepeatinn.co.uk
W www.thepeatinn.co.uk
Patricia & David Wilson

8 suites
From £165 per room per night
Dinner from £32

Open all year Tuesday-Saturday

From Edinburgh: take the M90 to Halbeath and the A92/A915 towards St Andrews. The Peat Inn is at the centre of the village of the same name.

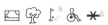

Foodies make a beeline for this terrific restaurant with rooms a short drive from St Andrews, where the pleasures of the table spill over into eight beautifully appointed split-level suites. Owners David and Patricia Wilson have extended this former Fife coaching inn to create comfortable guest quarters for diners keen to prolong their post-prandial pleasures. Chef Laureate David is also a past winner of the National Wine Awards – so guests are assured of some Bacchanalian high living. Diners tuck into fresh-landed lobster, crab, scallops and langoustines, prime Scotch beef and season's game. There's a remarkable wine list that won't break the bank either. Peaceful suites – each with its own roomy lounge, marble bathroom and quality aromatics – overlook rustic gardens, while good solid walls ensure utter privacy. But the restaurant is the real star of this friendly establishment in an inviting corner of Fife. Intimate tables provide a fetching setting for a dinner à deux.

Love time   Nights in white satin? Then tumble into the four-poster Floribunda suite.

Love bites   Menus are mouthwatering: choose from fillet of halibut with lobster risotto and herb sauce, or roast saddle of venison with a mushroom and truffle cake. Signature sweets include de-lish bitter chocolate tart.

Love it up   Fife's pretty fishing villages and coastal walks are close at hand, as are castles and National Trust gardens. And golfers are a mere strike from St Andrews' hallowed turf.

Who loves?   Lovebirds who adore their nosh almost as much as each other.

You'll love ♥   The serenity: guests have dubbed this the Inn of Great Happiness.

Rufflets Country House

Strathkinness Low Road, St Andrews
Fife KY16 9TX
T 01334 472594
F 01334 478703
E reservations@rufflets.co.uk
W www.rufflets.co.uk
Ann Murray-Smith
Ken Mathewson

20 rooms, 4 suites
£199 to £270 per room per night
Dinner from £36

Closed 2-14 Jan

From Edinburgh: take the M90/A92 towards Glenrothes and the Tay Bridge, then the A914/A91 to St Andrews. After Guardbridge turn right, following signs to Rufflets.

The centuries-old town of St Andrews is Scotland's answer to Oxford and Cambridge – but with a charm all of its own. One mile to the West, you'll find this gorgeous turreted country mansion, which has been welcoming guests since the 1920s when it started life as a grand private home. Since then, it's become one of Scotland's top ten luxury hotels, and a mecca not just for serious golfers but for lovers who wouldn't know a downswing from a divot. Interiors are sumptuously decorated, with original art, buttery-soft fabrics and sink-your-toes-in carpets. Many of the 24 rooms (there's also an exclusive-use lodge in the grounds) have canopied or four-poster beds and roomy whirlpool baths. Gardens are as immaculately manicured as the vainest coquette. You're just a short swing from the town's hallowed golfing fairways, and in the unlikely event of a lovers' tiff, Rufus the Rufflets teddy will keep you warm in bed.

Love time   Ask for Room Five – with its canopied bed and turreted seating area, this was recently voted Britain's most romantic bedroom.

Love bites   Modern Scottish cuisine is served in the Garden restaurant on candlelit tables set with fine china. Try seared collop of venison on dauphinoise potatoes, sautéed foie gras, fresh asparagus and raspberry tea syrup, and toast each other from a selection of over 100 wines.

Love it up   Try a spooky-wooky witches' tour of St Andrews – a great excuse for holding hands.

Who loves?   Emma Thompson, John Cleese and a host of top golfing names stay here.

You'll love   Fore! Could be just the place for some serious follow-through.

Roman Camp

off Main Street, Callander
Perthshire FK17 8BG
T 01877 330003
F 01877 331533
E mail@roman-camp-hotel.co.uk
W www.roman-camp-hotel.co.uk
Eric & Marion Brown

11 rooms, 3 suites
£125 to £185 per room per night
Dinner from £39

Open all year

Head North on the A84 to Callander.
From the main street, turn left down
a 300 yard drive between two pink
houses, into the hotel grounds.

Smart looking and prettily pink, Roman Camp was built as a hunting lodge for the Dukes of Perth. There was once an old Roman fort here, and get this, the clipped lawns of the hotel's tranquil 20 acres beside the River Teith have now been recognised as the turf where Roman centurions first played the forerunner to football. Nowadays it's owners Eric and Marion Brown who score the goals with deep comforts all round. Reception rooms with panelling and fires are opulently done up with rich fabrics and plump furnishings, while beds pursue the same sumptuousness. The spaciously configured Oval restaurant, hung with hand-stitched tapestries, has all the candlelit sophistication you could wish for. Chef Ian McNaught's repertoire is top-notch, with freshly-netted turbot and truffled langoustine or poulet noir breast with black pudding and prosciutto. Vegetarians take a good pass here too. Views from public areas and many bedrooms overlook the gardens and Perthshire's rolling beauty. The Browns have certainly embraced the Roman concept of civilisation; we were conquered.

Love time   Bedrooms are beautifully tricked out with sumptuous furnishings. You may choose to stay put right there.
Love bites   The spacious dining room is aglow with damask, silver and crystal. Choose between terrific tasting menus or à la carte.
Love it up   Check out some of Perthshire's pearls: take to the Trossachs and infamous Rob Roy country; scout around Stirling Castle or call into cute Callander.
Who loves?   Perthshire pleasure seekers.

You'll love   Going Roman in the gloamin.

SCOTLAND

Cromlix House

Kinbuck, by Dunblane
nr. Stirling FK15 9JT
T 01786 822125
F 01786 825450
E reservations@cromlixhouse.com
W www.cromlixhouse.com
David & Ailsa Assenti

6 rooms, 8 suites
£235 to £265 per room per night
Dinner from £30

Closed 2-25 Jan

From the A9: four miles north of
Dunblane (Stirling), take the B8033 to
Kinbuck. Cross the narrow bridge and
the drive is 200 yards on, on the left.

Captain Arthur Hay Drummond built Cromlix in 1874 as a substantial "cottage." The result was this opulent late Victorian mansion, now run as one of Scotland's most glamorous and feted country house hotels. Antiques, fine paintings, comfortable armchairs, the smell of log fires and mellow wood-panelled walls help preserve the air of an Edwardian family home. There are four different dining rooms to choose from. Does your taste turn to the solemnity of the ancestral library or the more feminine delights of the Green room? The luxury doesn't stop there, either: hedonistic bathrooms have fluffy robes and luxury toiletries and the eight sumptuous suites are vast enough for some playful hide-and-seek before tumbling into the outsize canopied brass beds.

Love time   The quirky Rapunzel-style Upper Turret room has a roll-top bath big enough for three.

Love bites   Dinner is a lavish affair, with crystal glinting in the candlelight. Unashamedly haute cuisine blends with Scottish tradition here in dishes such as fillet of Angus beef with potato rosti, spinach, lardons, shallots and a red wine jus. Fish dishes are delicious, too.

Love it up   A hearty breakfast will set you up for a hard day's play. The hotel can arrange salmon and trout fishing, clay pigeon shooting, off-road driving and falconry. Ten golf courses (including Gleneagles) are within an hour's drive.

Who loves?   Hearts fluttered here at the sight of Liam Neeson and Natasha Richardson. Eddie Izzard caused shock waves of an entirely different kind.

You'll love ▸ The fairytale private chapel – a perfect place to make or renew your vows.

Dalhousie Castle & Spa

Bonnyrigg, Edinburgh
EH19 3JB
T 01875 820153
F 01875 821936
E info@dalhousiecastle.co.uk
W www.dalhousiecastle.co.uk
Chris Ling

36 rooms, 2 suites
£120 to £325 per room per night
Dinner from £34

Open all year

From Edinburgh: take the A7 South, turning right at Shell garage on to the B704. The castle entrance is on the right (double back beneath road bridge) after half a mile.

A pink sandstone castle surrounded by wooded parkland, this 13th century fortress embodies the ultimate in Scottish legend, with a promise of good food, a warm welcome and plenty of tales within. Its guestlist, weighty with the names of kings and queens, and hidden nooks and crannies in the stone walls serve as reminders of its turbulent past. This is the ideal setting to re-enact your own yarns of passion and intrigue. Blend your romantic inspiration with the De Ramseia suite's seductive double jacuzzi and original stone well, mull over your plot with a book from the well stocked library, enjoy a wee dram from the secret bar by the hearth, or bliss out in the hydrotherapy Spa. Of course, if you like your stories to have a fairytale ending, the original private chapel is the best place to embark on a happy ever after.

Love time Go Gothic with love on the battlements: the Sir William Wallace room has doors opening onto the castle ramparts.

Love bites The auld alliance between Scots and French is celebrated in the candlelit barrel-vaulted dining room in the Dungeon restaurant.

Love it up Stroll through the grounds with a hooded hawk perched on your gauntlet. Nothing like a spot of falconry to bring out the hero in you.

Who loves? Queen Victoria stayed behind these ramparts, as did Sir Walter Scott. So too did Braveheart himself, William Wallace – though we don't know about Mel Gibson!

You'll love ❤ The Spa's passion fruit-scented tropical shower and aromatic Ottoman steam room.

The Witchery by the Castle

Castlehill, Royal Mile
Edinburgh EH1 2NF
T 0131 225 5613
F 0131 220 4392
E mail@thewitchery.com
W www.thewitchery.com
James Thomson

7 suites
£275 per suite per night including
breakfast in your suite and a
complimentary bottle of champagne
Dinner from £30

Closed 25-26 Dec

A five-minute taxi ride from Edinburgh's
Waverley station.

This wicked hedonist's heaven in the heart of Edinburgh (and winner of our Sexy Suites award) has been famously described as "the perfect lust den." Each of the seven extraordinary suites conspires to create an intoxicating setting, with acres of rampant velvet, extravagant tapestries, strewn cushions, glistening wood panelling and rich jewel colours. It's theatrical, atmospheric and gorgeously Gothic; no wonder celebs love it. Stuffed with Victorian curios and collectibles, opulent four-posters, gilded sofas, baronial portraits and polished antique floors, bedrooms are the stuff of fantasy. The Vestry is done out in dramatic red, gold and black, with a huge roll-top bath; the wood-panelled Guardroom has a tapestry-hung bed and views over Edinburgh's old town; the Inner Sanctum's lacquer-red bathroom has a wonderfully restored Victorian bath and shower; the Sempill suite boasts walls covered in antique leather and a four-poster hung with velvet, while the Old Rectory comes with a huge empire-style day bed. Mood-enhancing lighting, complimentary champagne and piles of CDs and DVDs complete the idyll. Phew.

Love time Visiting stars rate the Inner Sanctum, with its raised dining dais and antique-crammed Victorian bathroom.
Love bites There's serious prize-winning cuisine: try pan-roasted wild sea bass, seared Skye scallops or monkfish en papillotte. Follow with the suite course...
Love it up All Edinburgh awaits: you're right on the castle-crowned Royal Mile.
Who loves? Michael Douglas and Catherine Zeta Jones have stayed, as has bad boy Jack Nicholson.

You'll love ▶ Romantic panache from the rafters down.

Royal Mile Residence

219 Royal Mile, Edinburgh
EH1 1PE
T 0131 226 5155
F 0131 477 4636
E info@royalmileresidence.com
W www.royalmileresidence.com
Jacqui King

7 apartments
1 bed apartment: £150 to £225 per night
2 bed apartment: £175 to £300 per night

Open all year

A five-minute taxi ride from Edinburgh's
Waverley station.

Billed as the city's newest private pied à terre, Royal Mile Residence could be just the place to shut out the outside world, with the buzz of the Royal Mile on your doorstep. Offering a stylish alternative to traditional hotel stays (the spartan stone staircase leaves arriving guests unprepared for the plush interiors within), its six serviced apartments are tucked inside a four-storey Georgian building that was once home to Elsie Inglis, pioneering doctor and women's rights advocate. Surroundings are ultra-sleek with splashes of tartan and deep hues of chocolate and aubergine on the walls. Bedrooms have luxury double or twin beds and apartments are kitted out with a wide-screen TV, internet access and DVD player. Fill the fridge with bubbly, kick off your shoes for a lazy night in after a day's sightseeing and dress (or undress) for dinner as you please. All guests enjoy full use of the gym and spa facilities at the nearby Escape health club. So for a spot of his-and-hers pampering, book in for one of their many spa treatments to help you relax and unwind.

Love time   Take one of the front apartments to watch the Royal Mile come to life after dark.

Love bites   Play at being a domestic goddess (or god) in your own fully fitted kitchen, order in a takeaway or try one of the Royal Mile's many eateries.

Love it up   Stroll to Edinburgh Castle or Holyrood Palace, have a wee dram at the Scotch Whisky Heritage Centre or try a breezy open-top bus tour.

Who loves?   Metropolitan types who like their own front door key.

You'll love   Home-from-home privacy in a capital designer nest.

SCOTLAND

Prestonfield

Priestfield Road, Edinburgh
EH16 5UT
T 0131 225 7800
F 0131 220 4392
E reservations@prestonfield.com
W www.prestonfield.com
James Thomson

22 rooms, 2 suites
From £195 per room per night
including full Scottish breakfast and a
complimentary bottle of champagne
Dinner from £35

Open all year

From city centre (ten mins):
join the Dalkeith Road,
turning left into Priestfield Road after
the Royal Commonwealth Pool.

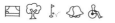

Prestonfield has been billed as the ultimate retort to minimalism. Think full-on theatrical Baroque here: expect to be stopped in your tracks. Multi-million pound refurbishment of this 17th century mansion on Edinburgh's edge puts words like opulent and decadent in the shade. It's visual high drama from the word go: backdrops of velvet-upholstered walls and panelling, extravagant damask sofas, lavishly swagged and draped burgundy brocades, leopardskin throws and candelabra. Regency furniture is ornate, artefacts are quixotic, flower arrangements are glorious; gilded flourishes abound. It's enough to make modernists blanch, and it pulls together superbly. Bedrooms are no less flamboyant: luxurious Frette sheets lie alongside broadband, Bose wave sound, DVD players and plasma screens. Guests can chill in various beautiful salons splashed in scarlet, gold and black and scented by tuberose. Linger over cocktails before dining in the chandeliered Rhubarb restaurant, or arrange an intimate assignation in one of three other private dining rooms. Prestonfield isn't all show either: this shamelessly OTT pleasure palace has been officially awarded five stars.

Love time   Bedrooms resemble boudoirs on a Gothic film set. Behind closed doors, rooms ooze sex appeal alongside top technics.
Love bites   Rhubarb chef Kenny Coltman's seductive Black Gold beef is pure "eat me!"
Love it up   Explore the estate's 20 acres before raiding Edinburgh's chic George Street.
Who loves?   Style bible Tatler calls Prestonfield "rich, ripe, almost dissolute." "Fabulous!" says Joan Collins.

You'll love ❥ Baroque extravaganza packed with the Wow factor.

The Royal Scotsman

46a Constitution Street
Edinburgh EH6 6RS
T 0131 555 1021
F 0131 555 1345
E enquiries@royalscotsman.co.uk
W www.royalscotsman.com
Francesca Snitjer

20 cabins
From £610 per person per night
Fully inclusive

Operates May – October

Departures from Edinburgh's Waverley station, where guests have use of the first class lounge.

The Royal Scotsman is sheer romance on rails – a luxury rolling country house party for those keen to enjoy glorious scenery and mouthwatering cuisine in shameless comfort. Guests are piped on board, then whisked back to the lavish golden age of rail travel in polished burgundy-crested coaches. Watch the unfolding panorama of scenic glens and heather-covered hills outside from the Edwardian Observation Car lined with tartan sofas, then join fellow guests for a convivial dinner amid the velvet and candelabra-lit splendour of the dining cars. Places to visit range from the Gothic splendour of Victorian Mount Stuart and turreted Ballindalloch Castle to the Highland Wildlife Park. You'll sleep like a king, stabled for the night in a quiet siding or station. Itineraries range from the Wee Dram one-nighter to the four-night Classic taking in Kyle of Lochalsh and some of Scotland's most jaw-dropping scenery. Getting wanderlust? Your carriage awaits.

Love time Bijou cabins (twin-bedded, but who cares?) come with mahogany panelling, crisp linen sheets and private facilities.

Love bites There's a gold-star gourmet restaurant on board: guests dine on escalope of wild salmon, fillet of Aberdeen Angus beef and fairy-light soufflés. All drinks, down to that umpteenth (hic) glass of bubbly, are included.

Love it up Daytime excursions are followed by lively after-dinner entertainment: look forward to kilted storytellers, local fiddlers or a foot-tapping ceilidh.

Who loves? Luxury train aficionados. "So romantic you'll want to throw yourself off," sighed one. We'd rather you didn't!

You'll love ♥ The grandest of Highland flings.

The Howard

34 Great King Street
Edinburgh EH3 6QH
T 0131 557 3500
F 0131 557 6515
E reserve@thehoward.com
W www.thehoward.com
Johanne Falconer

18 rooms, 5 suites
£180 to £395 per room per night
Dinner from £30

Closed 25-28 Dec

A five-minute taxi ride from Waverley
station and eight miles from
Edinburgh Airport.

Two's company, three is gracious living. Leave the cases in the car. Your private butler will whisk them in for you and unpack as you take tea in the drawing room. Soak up the elegance of Edinburgh's New Town in this handsome 1820s row of Georgian townhouses. Just ask your butler to run a bath, draw the curtains or even serve dinner in your room, and to withdraw when it's time to batten down. With high ceilings and views of the Firth of Forth from the damask- and brocade-swathed sash windows, the Howard's aristocratic chic is accentuated by a dramatic sweeping staircase, antique furnishings and oil paintings. Style and comfort are not frozen in the past, either, and rooms (each bearing a name rather than a number), boast DVDs and internet access. The low-tech stuff is great too: the bathroom in Lauriston is pampering central with Floris toiletries and a huge free-standing bathtub to share. Come here for the amenities of a top hotel and the intimacy of a personal pied à terre in one of Britain's great cities.

Love time	The King suite has its own private front door onto the cobbled street outside – so no-one need know how late you get home.
Love bites	The Atholl restaurant is five-star dining at its best, with hallmark modern Scottish dishes including saffron-spiced monkfish tail. And it would be a sin to miss afternoon tea here: finger sandwiches, home-baked scones, scrumptious éclairs and wicked chocolate tiffin.
Love it up	Give your platinum a workout in Princes Street or stroll the Royal Mile.
Who loves?	Think 007 – Sean Connery, the original Bond, hails from this city.
You'll love ♥	The butler. Champers, anyone?

NORTH

Go for Yorkshire Dales, lakeland vales
Eat fish and chips in a newspaper
Take blissful massage oils – for post-walk pampering
Bedtime story? Emily Brontë: *Wuthering Heights*

Berwick-upon-Tweed

55

A69

Carlisle

54

Newcastle-upon-Tyne

Durham

Cockermouth

53

52

Penrith

49

Middlesbrough

A595

51

50

Windermere

M6

48

Scarborough

47

A1

York

Blackpool

M55

M65

Bradford

Hull

M57

M62

Manchester

Doncaster

Liverpool

Sheffield

46

45

Chester

44

Pages 44-55

Frogg Manor

Nantwich Road
Broxton, Chester CH3 9JH
T 01829 782629
F 01829 782459
E info@froggmanorhotel.co.uk
W www.froggmanorhotel.co.uk
John Sykes

5 rooms, 2 suites
£80 to £200 per room per night
Dinner from £25

Open all year

From the M54 (J3): take the A41
North. Turn right on
the A534 (signed Nantwich). Drive
past Frogg Manor and take the first
turning right. The entrance is then
on the right.

Froggie would a-wooing go… and here's just the place to do it. This unashamedly eccentric home offers the unlikely combination of plush surroundings, old-time music… and frogs. Hundreds of them (fortunately made of wood, ceramic, brass and straw) cluster round the place, while a human-size frog in a polka-dot tie points guests the way in. Don't like amphibians? Then this probably isn't the place for you. Owner John Sykes (who admits to being just mildly croaky), has created an anything-but-bourgeois country house environment with a pleasing mix of period furniture, generous floral displays and pastel colours. Windows are tasselled, draped and flounced, bedrooms are lavishly done up with Egyptian cotton sheets, while bathrooms come packed with goodies. Floodlit landscaped gardens give way to rolling Cheshire and the Welsh hills. John supervises the kitchen and guests can tuck into some 24 starters (including incomparable Froggie fishcakes) and over 30 mains (try more-ish cream of Zanzibar bouillabaisse) with vegetarians getting a good look-in too. There's a jukebox in the bar (but no karaoke), and a party room for after-dinner dancing to '50s classics.

Love time Dive into the coronet-swathed bed in the middle of the Wellington suite.
Love bites Cosmopolitan inspired dishes are cooked with flair; the prime Beef Wellington is just right for sharing.
Love it up Play tennis, trawl through Chester's groovy stores or explore Cheshire's rolling hills and villages.
Who loves? Miss Froggies in search of their prince.

You'll love ❤ Some very kissable froggs!

Broxton Hall

Whitchurch Road, Broxton
Chester CH3 9JS
T 01829 782321
F 01829 782330
E reservations@broxtonhall.co.uk
W www.broxtonhall.co.uk
The Ireland family

10 rooms
£80 to £130 per room per night
Dinner from £32

Open all year

From Chester: take the A41, signposted Whitchurch. Cross the A534 after nine miles and the hotel is just ahead on your left.

With its black and white half-timbered Tudor frontage, Broxton Hall looks just the kind of place where kings and queens of old might have tarried for a sporting country weekend. These days you can enjoy country sport of another kind in this charismatic Jacobean manor house, with its rich wood-panelled walls, plush beds, antique furnishings and huge fireplace where logs crackle merrily on a winter's night. An impressive (and authentically creaky) carved mahogany staircase leads upstairs to the ten guestrooms, beautifully furnished with antiques and cosy lamps. Chef Chris Ireland's consistently praised French-English cooking combines flavour with flair in the pretty dining room, where tall candlesticks and service add finesse. Breakfast is taken in the sunny conservatory, while drinks are served on the terrace in warm weather. With its Tudor beamed exterior, Broxton Hall would look right at home in the walled city of Chester, and sure enough, you're just ten miles from its buzzy boutiques and ancient cathedral.

Love time	Book the four-poster Bridal suite, with its ornately carved bed, rich colours and drapes. All rooms are well appointed, with every modern comfort.
Love bites	Try Cumbrian cured ham, followed by delicious roast Cheshire duckling and rounded off with crepes flambéed in Cointreau and orange sauce.
Love it up	Historic Chester is on the doorstep, not to mention the mountains of Snowdonia. Pick a winner at the Chester or Bangor-on-Dee races, play golf or visit 1,000 acre Tatton Park, with its herds of red and fallow deer.
Who loves?	First-nighters, race-goers and Chester weekenders.
You'll love	Plenty of Cheshire charm: old-time ambience and new-age comforts.

White House Manor

The Village, Prestbury
Cheshire SK10 4HP
T 01625 829376
F 01625 828627
E info@thewhitehouse.uk.com
W www.thewhitehouse.uk.com
Ryland & Judith Wakeham

11 rooms
£80 to £130 per room per night
Dinner from £18.95

Closed Christmas

From the M6 (J17): take the A534 towards Congleton, then the A536 to Prestbury. White House Manor is located just over the bridge.

Owners Ryland and Judith Wakeham have infused this Cheshire Georgian manor house with oodles of contemporary style. Eleven brilliantly conceived bedrooms let guests choose from the sensuous to the traditional, and the fantastical to the downright decadent. Feeling naughty? There's the Crystal room, with its stunning chandelier, new whirlpool bath and tile TV; opulent Aphrodite (a real lovers' lair); Campion, whose four-poster is swathed in chiffon; scarlet-and-gold themed Minerva; and the Coach House – all muted browns and sultry golds, with a state-of-the art bathroom and its own private entrance. Individual pieces of art, furniture and collectibles have been chosen with consummate care to create sumptuous private sanctuaries perfect for putting up the Do Not Disturb sign.

Love time   The futuristic Millennium room boasts a glass bed and wicked Turkish steam room – a 21st century harem for two.

Love bites   Modern British cuisine is served with continental flair. Try the assiette of goat's cheese, followed by the grilled sea bass with risotto nero and champagne lime sauce. Sweet tooths should get stuck into Ryland's plate of British desserts for sharing (we loved the melting chocolate fondant).

Love it up   Hit the shops in happening Manchester, or get out and explore some of the region's great aristocratic country seats at Tatton, Chatsworth, Lyme Park and Styal.

Who loves?   Honeymooners adore this extravagantly romantic haven.

You'll love   Suite serenity – serious style, fabulous food, and you.

Austwick Traddock

Austwick, via Lancaster
North Yorkshire LA2 8BY
T 015242 51224
F 015242 51796
E info@austwicktraddock.co.uk
W www.austwicktraddock.co.uk
Bruce & Jane Reynolds

10 rooms
£100 to £140 per room per night
Dinner from £23

Open all year

From Skipton: take the A65 towards
Kendal, turning right to Austwick
approx two miles after Settle.

How did this creeper-clad Georgian country house set in the heart-stopping beauty of the Yorkshire Dales get its name? Apparently it derives from the trade that used to take place in the paddock overlooked by the hotel grounds in the pretty village of Austwick – hence Traddock. Now you know. But its distinctive name is not the only thing that makes this characterful place stand out from the crowd. Sofas made for sinking into and crackling fires lend its antique-furnished interior a welcoming warmth, making it a favourite with locals, walkers and those touring the Dales. Individually decorated bedrooms are stylishly done out with all the home-from-home touches you could want – not to mention bucolic views of the landscape. Be sure to bring a hearty appetite to dinner – this is an ace award-winning kitchen, and dishes major on using season's best local – and organic – ingredients. Outside, the air is fresh enough to bottle, so you'll want to hit those walking trails or take to the outdoor terrace in summer.

Love time Room 11 – secluded and spacious – is a fave with honeymooners.
Love bites Blackboard menus feature new takes on old favourites. Try a Dales fillet steak with dauphinoise potato, caramelised banana shallots and Madeira sauce, followed by rhubarb compote with crumble and bay leaf custard.
Love it up You're on the doorstep of Brontë and Herriot country, while spectacular walking trails start right here. Feeling lazy? Let the scenery come to you with a ride on the famous Settle to Carlisle railway.
Who loves? Fresh air fans who adore their home comforts.

You'll love An out-and-out Dales delight.

The Blue Lion

East Witton, nr. Leyburn
North Yorkshire DL8 4SN
T 01969 624273
F 01969 624189
E bluelion@breathemail.net
W www.thebluelion.co.uk
Paul & Helen Klein

12 rooms
£69 to £89 per room per night
Dinner from £22.50

Open all year

From the A1 and South: take the B6267 north of Dishforth towards Masham. Follow the A6108 past Masham and continue to East Witton.

Step back in time at this 18th century coaching inn, which mixes the traditions of a country pub with the feel of a period home. Set in the heart of Wensleydale, the stone-built Blue Lion draws locals and visitors alike. Old-fashioned comfort and charm is the keynote here, with plenty of stripped wood, flagstone floors and shuttered windows. Old sporting prints, rustic bric-a-brac and ham hooks decked with sheaves of corn help set the tone in the bar, with its high-backed settles and Windsor chairs. Sizzling log fires and polished bar taps positively encourage lazing over the papers with a pint of hand-pulled real ale. The 12 bedrooms – recently perked up by owners Paul and Helen Klein – are individually decorated with dark wood furniture, pleasing colours, country-floral fabrics and old prints. The candlelit restaurant, with its picture-covered walls, apron-clad waiters and chalk board menus, has won a string of culinary awards, making this a mecca for foodies.

Love time   Choose between the olde-time charm of rooms in the inn (creaky floorboards included) or beamed ceilings and pine in the newer stables.

Love bites   Chef John Dalby puts the focus firmly on fresh local game and fish. Tuck into traditional roasts and delicious puds.

Love it up   This is walking, fishing and shooting country, so get out and enjoy the Dales. Take a twilight trip to the ruins of Jervaulx Abbey or head off to the Minster and cobbled-street Shambles of York.

Who loves?   HRH Prince Charles – who dined here two nights running.

You'll love   Top-notch cooking and country pub charm.

The Rose & Crown

Romaldkirk, Barnard Castle
County Durham DL12 9EB
T 01833 650213
F 01833 650828
E hotel@rose-and-crown.co.uk
W www.rose-and-crown.co.uk
Christopher & Alison Davy

12 rooms
£110 to £130 per room per night
Dinner from £26

Closed Christmas

From the A1: take the A66 to Bowes, then take road to Barnard Castle. The hotel is six miles north-west of Barnard Castle on the B6277.

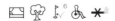

Of the hundreds of Rose & Crowns in Britain, this one is the tops. A visibly loved 18th century coaching inn is crowned by its location in Romaldkirk, a pretty conservation village complete with stocks and green twixt Teesdale's fells and moors. It's kept to perfection; all beams, brasses, glowing copper and polished panelling. Exposed brickwork, cosy snugs, dancing fires in the grate and the reassuring tick of a grandfather clock create more atmosphere in the bar, where locals are likely to sweep you up in Northern friendliness. There's elegance, too. Expect starched napery and silver candlesticks in the oak-panelled dining room or red walls and framed cartoons in the brasserie. Discerning palates make a beeline here for chef Andrew Lee's first-rate gastropub cuisine, showered with awards. New on the menu is a creamy Yorkshire Blue, spinach and pancetta risotto (eat your heart out Gordon Ramsay). Bedrooms are newly revamped, and stylishly decorated with eye-catching details while enjoying village-green views. There are also courtyard rooms where pet pooches are welcome. Hands-on owners Christopher and Alison Davy provide hospitality with great good humour.

Love time	Rustic beams, half-testers and feathery pillows set the tone for beddy-byes.
Love bites	Scrumptious fare includes pink roast fillet of Teesdale fell lamb with woodland mushroom and potato broth, and sticky butterscotch pudding.
Love it up	Head updale to High Force, England's highest waterfall, wild moorlands, turreted Raby Castle or the cathedral city of Durham.
Who loves?	Many an English rose and her swain.
You'll love	Cute and cosy has never been this chic.

Linthwaite House

Crook Road, Bowness-on-Windermere
LA23 3JA
T 015394 88600
F 015394 88601
E admin@linthwaite.com
W www.linthwaite.com
Mike Bevans

27 rooms
£150 to £295 per room per night
Dinner from £42

Open all year

From M6 (J36): take dual carriageway (past Kendal) for eight miles. At the roundabout north-west of Kendal, take the first exit (B5284) signed Crook. The hotel is on the left after seven miles.

"Aah, the Lake District…" as Wordsworth didn't quite say. But we have to say this Edwardian hilltop hotel is one to rhapsodise over, with its dreamy views over Lake Windermere. The interior has been stylishly done out by Amanda Rosa (of Malmaison fame), so don't expect acres of frou-frou and frills. The traditional framework has been zooted up with a contemporary palette of colours and fabrics. There are unfussy antiques and bare wooden floors, kilims, leather trunk coffee tables and colonial rattan chairs in the conservatory. It all marries together nicely. (Indeed, the clockwork running of the hotel and its lush 14-acre gardens make it perfect for nuptials). Two pretty dining rooms have walls strewn with mirrors that reflect flickering candlelight at night. Better still, chef Simon Bolsover's cooking is worth reflecting on – he's won plaudits from food critics galore. The terrace, with its lake and mountain vistas, adds pleasure to meals in good weather. Edwardians were stuffy, but this is far from it. So why wait?

Love time — Room 29 is the contender for most romantic room, while the Garden suite has a fab bathroom and views.

Love bites — Superb daily-changing menus might feature seared scallops, Goosenargh duck breast or wicked chocolate fondant. Yum.

Love it up — Picnic (or fish) by a private tarn, play croquet, chug across the lake by steamer or discover the homes of Wordsworth and Beatrix Potter.

Who loves? — Suitors about to pop the question. Staff will even pop champers and strawberries into the hotel's private summerhouse for the big moment.

You'll love ♥ — Ralph Lauren meets Raffles at this stylish lakeside address.

Holbeck Ghyll

Holbeck Lane, Windermere
Cumbria, LA23 1LU
T 015394 32375
F 015394 34743
E stay@holbeckghyll.com
W www.holbeckghyll.com
David & Patricia Nicholson

20 rooms
£220 to £350 per room per night
Michelin star dinner included

Open all year

From the M6 (J36): take the A591 to
Windermere, and continue towards
Ambleside. Turn right after three miles
into Holbeck Lane. The hotel is
half a mile further on the left.

Room for Romance readers' choice for our 2003 Hotel of the Year, this former Victorian hunting lodge more than lives up to its accolades. Poetic views, a to-die-for location overlooking Lake Windermere and the Langdale fells, a Michelin-starred restaurant and pocket-sized bijou spa (hot stone therapy is a must-try), make this lakeland jewel ripple with old-time romance. Plush decor, sumptuous sofas, warm wood panelling and sizzling fires invite guests to simply relax. Proprietors David and Patricia Nicholson are every bit as charming as their hotel, and the friendly but discreet service has helped earn them a hatful of awards. It's a haven for wildlife, too: jog around the grounds and you could spot deer, red squirrels and birds.

Love time   Be happy bunnies in Peter Rabbit in the Lodge, the honeymoon and anniversary suite. This lovenest extraordinaire has a roomy four-poster, a bath big enough for two, and sensational lake views.

Love bites   Dine outside in fine weather, or bag a window table and soak up lake and mountain vistas as you feast on roast quail with onion compote and truffle jus or a pillow of sea bass on puy lentils, braised salsify and jus sauterne.

Love it up   Visit in summer for golf, boating, fishing and wonderful walks. In winter, just curl up by the fire with a good book.

Who loves?   Screen heartthrob Ralph Fiennes described Holbeck Ghyll as "gorgeous." And he should know.

You'll love ❧   The place favoured by loved-up celebs, some of whom never step outside their suites. Bless!

Rampsbeck Country House

Watermillock, Ullswater
Cumbria CA11 0LP
T 01768 486442
F 01768 486688
E enquiries@rampsbeck.fsnet.co.uk
W www.rampsbeck.fsnet.co.uk
Marion Gibb

18 rooms, 1 suite
£140 to £250 per room per night
Dinner from £39

Closed 3 Jan – 9 Feb

From the M6 (J40): take the A66. Turn left on to the A592 for Watermillock.

You'll be penning rhyming couplets within minutes of arriving on the shores of Lake Ullswater – at least that's what happened to Wordsworth! Even if you don't succumb to verse, this comfortable hotel really is something to write home about. It's an elegant white-walled 18th century house, with drop-dead gorgeous views over the lake and fells, standing in 18 acres of lovingly tended gardens (a sea of dancing daffodils in spring, of course) and rolling parkland. Spacious salons are country-house trad – wood panelled walls, carved fireplaces and ornate plasterwork – with huge bay windows, a sweeping staircase and touches of modern elegance. Impressive dinner menus in the smart restaurant might feature pan-fried loin of hare, roasted squab or delicious Barbary duck. This is very much a family affair, run without a hint of stuffiness by lively husband and wife team Tom and Marion Gibb together with Marion's mother, Mrs MacDowell. By the time you leave, you'll feel like old friends.

Love time   Three rooms have a private balcony – perfect for sipping a sundowner.
Love bites   Succumb to the freshly-baked hot Valrhona chocolate fondant with black cherry and kirsch ice cream – it's worth the wait. In fine weather, enjoy a light meal on the terrace looking out at those poetic views.
Love it up   Up-for-it couples can enjoy golf, pony trekking, archery, mountain biking and clay pigeon shooting in the surrounds.
Who loves?   Savvy Lakeland travellers who know where to find relaxed, professional service – and great kippers.

You'll love   Being right on the lake, but far from the crowds – heaven.

The Pheasant

Bassenthwaite Lake
Nr. Cockermouth, Cumbria CA13 9YE
T 017687 76234
F 017687 76002
E info@the-pheasant.co.uk
W www.the-pheasant.co.uk
Matthew Wylie

15 rooms, 3 suites
£120 to £190 per room per night
Dinner from £27.95

Closed Christmas Day

From the M6 (J40): take the A66 for
Keswick. Head towards Cockermouth
and follow signs
on the A66.

No wonder guests fly back to the Pheasant year after year. This one-time farm became a coaching inn in 1778 and has been a haven of warmth and welcome ever since. It's a beautifully maintained building with 40 acres of grounds including a charming small garden. The mellow bar – all oak settles, polished walls, wooden beams, gleaming knick-knacks and log fires – has all the patina of a time-warp Lakeland hostelry. Bedrooms are pretty, fresh and filled with flowers, with old pine furniture, soft colours, lovely country fabrics and upmarket bathrooms stocked with quality smellies. Chef Malcolm Ennis's traditional fare flirts agreeably with modern cuisine, and dishes look as good on the plate as they taste. Regulars come here from miles around for dinner, dropping in during the day for scrumptious afternoon teas complete with cucumber sandwiches and home-baked scones with rum butter.

Love time Try the spacious four-postered Ennerdale suite. Whichever room you choose, staff will bring you early-morning tea in bed.

Love bites Dine on local Cumbrian specialities with a contemporary twist, such as pan-roasted pheasant and baby vegetables with wild mushrooms.

Love it up Get the wind in your sails along Bassenthwaite Lake and Derwent Water, or don your hiking boots and head for the fells. Pretty villages, antique shops and tearooms abound in this unspoilt end of the Lake District.

Who loves? Famous huntsman John Peel was a regular in the 19th century. We suspect he'd be happy to unpeel here again today.

You'll love Cumbrian conviviality mixed with country-house style comfort.

Lovelady Shield

Alston, Cumbria CA9 3LF
T 01434 381203
F 01434 381515
E enquiries@lovelady.co.uk
W www.lovelady.co.uk
Peter & Marie Haynes

12 rooms
£140 to £240 per room per night
Dinner from £35.50

Open all year

From the M6 (J40): take the A66 eastbound, then the A686 to Alston. The hotel entrance is at the junction of the A689 (at top of Alston's cobbled High Street) and B6294.

RR

Named by an anonymous 14th century landowner after the love of his life, Lovelady Shield has a pretty romantic ring to it – and the secluded driveway, through three acres of gardens, is a clue that you are in for a rare treat. Nudging England's highest market town, this pretty Georgian house is set amid the rolling fells of the High Pennines, on the banks of the River Nent, shielded by woods and hills. For friendly owners Peter and Marie Haynes, their hotel is palpably a labour of love, and the welcome is warm and friendly. In the elegant bar, library and lounge, with their crackling log fires and ticking clocks, conversation is convivial. Bedrooms in the 1950s extension have a more contemporary feel, while those in the main house are more traditional but all are supremely comfortable, with marble bathrooms. Many have stunning views across the valleys to the majestic Cumbrian fells.

Love time   Room Two is a fantasy in cream and silk, while Nine has a traditional four-poster and splashes of Scottish Black Watch tartan.

Love bites   Chef Barrie Gordon's award-winning British cooking with continental influences features imaginative dishes such as Stilton fritters in a piquant white onion sauce, Lune Valley lamb and fig sponge pudding.

Love it up   Explore the Pennines, the Yorkshire Dales and Hadrian's Wall. For a steamy affair, try the South Tynedale railway; for soul food – Durham Cathedral.

Who loves?   Lovers and their ladies. Famous names to drop in here include the Blairs, actress Lindsay Duncan and Janet Street-Porter.

You'll love   Old-fashioned hospitality miles from the urban rush.

NORTH

Waren House Hotel

Waren Mill, Belford
Northumberland NE70 7EE
T 01668 214581
F 01668 214484
E enquires@warenhousehotel.co.uk
W www.warenhousehotel.co.uk
Peter & Anita Laverack

8 rooms, 4 suites
£130 to £205 per room per night
Dinner from £22.50

Open all year

From the A1: take the B1342 towards Bamburgh. Turn right at the T-junction in the village of Waren Mill.

Hordes would descend if they knew about Peter and Anita Laverack's Northumberland gem with its sweeping views across Budle Bay to the Holy Island of Lindisfarne. This charming Georgian house, with its six acres of wooded grounds, sits sheltered from the Cheviot Hills just a few miles from Bamburgh and its famous castle. Not that this is simply a peaceful country home. Step inside the flamboyant entrance hall, and you'll feel you have walked into a colourfully eccentric antique emporium, crammed with Victorian dolls of every shape and size. Ornaments and bric-a-brac, gilded antique mirrors, oriental rugs, rich terracotta walls and a cheerful log fire all add to the distinct sense of style. The leather-covered easy chairs in the drawing room are just the place to gaze out at the freshly stocked walled garden outside, while upstairs, individually decorated bedrooms are all charmers.

Love time You're spoiled for choice here. There's the Gray suite, with its muted tones and four-poster; The Maria suite, decked out in panelling from an old Welsh chapel; and the pretty Edwardian suite.

Love bites Expect the best of modern Northumbrian cuisine, whether it's poached rainbow trout, baked salmon in a mussel soup or sinful gypsy tart. An impressive wine list runs to some 250 bins.

Love it up Stroll the dunes of Budle Bay, take the low-tide causeway to Lindisfarne, check out Bamburgh castle or head for the heart of scenic Northumberland.

Who loves? No-one's saying. This is in the Secret Kingdom, after all...

You'll love A northern star just a stone's throw from Holy Island.

MIDSHIRES

Go for potteries, parks and plays by the Bard
Eat a roast with all the trimmings
Take something frolicsome (for making merry)
Bedtime story? DH Lawrence: *Lady Chatterley's Lover*

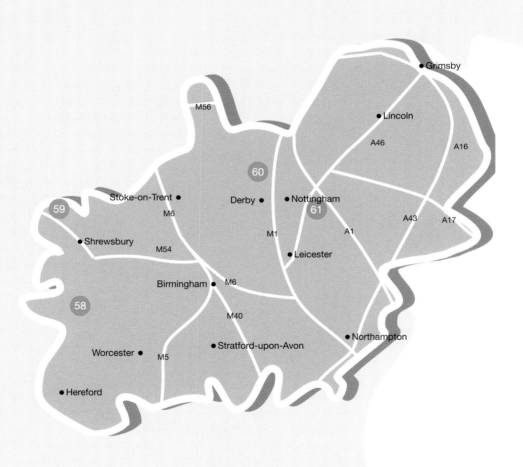

Pages 58-61

Hundred House Hotel

Bridgnorth Road, Norton, nr. Shifnal
Shropshire TF11 9EE
T 01952 730353
F 01952 730355
E reservations@hundredhouse.co.uk
W www.hundredhouse.co.uk
The Phillips family

10 rooms
£99 to £135 per room per night
Dinner from £25

Open all year

From the M54 (J4): take the A442
past Telford, directly to Norton.

We've seen a few four-poster beds, quirky pictures and characterful flourishes in our time, but finding a velvet-covered swing in our room was something new. Still, that's exactly what you can expect at Hundred House Hotel, where swinging from the rafters is absolutely de rigueur. Once the novelty wears off, pause to take in the boudoir charms of lavender-scented pillowcases and four-poster or brass beds made for bouncing into. Pretty patchwork drapes, deep colours, stencilling and period furniture all add to the appeal. But it's not just the bedrooms that make this old Shropshire inn a real charmer. Eclectic art, old brick walls, beamed ceilings, sheaves of dried herbs and bold colours mark out a place that revels in being different. Owners the Phillips family happily admit to a tad of eccentricity – evidenced from the moment you walk in and see the big Temperance Hall sign downstairs. (No worries, you'll soon have a drink in your hand). We'd give this hospitable hostelry high marks out of a hundred.

Love time   It's playtime for grown-ups here, with a full-size bedroom swing waiting for you to twirl around in.

Love bites   Dine in the warren of inter-connecting dining rooms, where blackboard menus flag up dishes that have showered the kitchen in culinary awards. How about beef and venison casserole with bacon and herb dumplings? Breakfast shines with home-made jams and jellies.

Love it up   You're close to historic Shrewsbury here, and the hilly Welsh Marches.

Who loves?   Lovebirds after a swinging time.

You'll love ❤   A house with a hundredfold charms.

MIDSHIRES

Pen-y-Dyffryn

Rhydycroesau, Oswestry
Shropshire SY10 7JD
T 01691 653700
F 01691 650066
E stay@peny.co.uk
W www.peny.co.uk
Mike Whetton

12 rooms
£100 to £160 per room per night
Dinner from £31.50

Closed 20 Dec – 20 Jan

From the M54: continue along the A5
to Oswestry, then follow signs to
Llansilin on the B4580 through
Oswestry town centre.

It's chocolate-box lovely here, perched 1,000 feet up on Shropshire's last hill, gazing westwards over a swathe of green towards the mountains of the Welsh borders. This multiple award-winning hotel – a silver stone Georgian house with five acres of cultivated gardens and a little stream – exudes the tranquillity stressed townies crave. Only wildlife breaks the silence. It's charmingly decorated: antiques, log fires, big comfy chairs, fresh flowers and prettily decorated bedrooms, some with spa baths. Food, much of it locally sourced and organic, plays a key role. There's an extensive, modestly priced wine list, majoring on the New World and with many champagnes too. Cuisine is adventurous, and bursting with flavour. A terrace is laid for tea, or cocktails in clement weather. New owner Mike Whetton imbues this country hotel with a palpable sense of hospitality and warmth.

Love time	The Superior bedroom boasts a Japanese-style bathroom with jacuzzi. The adjacent Coach House enjoys private patios and views all round.
Love bites	Locally sourced ingredients provide prize fare. Look forward to spiced parsnip and apple soup, rack of Welsh salt-marsh lamb, game, honeycomb ice cream or Welsh cheeses.
Love it up	Splendid countryside encourages hill-walking or riding. Visit National Trust properties and medieval towns or go golfing and trout fishing.
Who loves?	Country lovers who can keep a secret.
You'll love ➤	"A retreat so peaceful it's a crime to publicise it," as one guest said. We'd gladly serve time here.

Riber Hall

Matlock, Derbyshire DE4 5JU
T 01629 582795
F 01629 580475
E info@riber-hall.co.uk
W www.riber-hall.co.uk
Alex Biggin

14 rooms
£136 to £182 per room per night
3 course dinner from £37

Closed Christmas Day

From the M1 (J28): take the A38 (signed Matlock) for three miles, then the A615 for seven miles to Tansley. From there, Alders Lane winds towards Riber Hall.

✱ RR

Over 30 years ago, Alex Biggin found this historic but derelict 16th century Derbyshire manor house set amid orchards and buttercup meadows in the rolling foothills of the Pennines. He fell in love, and breathed new life into its soft pink stonework and mullioned windows, creating gardens of rare and exotic plants – a dreamy place for a peaceful stroll, with no-one but the birds to eavesdrop. Charming period furnishings, from draped Georgian curtains to medieval heraldic symbols, have been harmoniously blended with modern comforts. Many rooms in the old hall and around the courtyard have whirlpool baths and four-poster beds. Staff will happily slip a hot water bottle under the covers for you, though we trust passion renders this unnecessary.

Love time A browse through the visitor's book here reveals all: references to handcuffs, steamy sessions in a four-poster bed and a lover who accidentally put her foot through the wooden headboard had us blushing. Must be something in the air here.

Love bites French provincial menus are pure gastroporn. Drool over hand-dived seared sea scallops with a crispy tomato and basil tart, buttered spinach and a balsamic dressing, or cappuccino semi-freddo with a home-made cinnamon doughnut. An award-winning wine list, too.

Love it up Explore the area's famous caverns and lakes, potter around local potteries, or visually plunder the great halls of Chatsworth and Haddon.

Who loves? Sting, Faye Dunaway, Julie Christie, Charlie Watts and (yes) Basil Brush.

You'll love Naughty nights in rural tranquillity.

Langar Hall

Langar, Nottinghamshire NG13 9HG
T 01949 860559
F 01949 861045
E info@langarhall.co.uk
W www.langarhall.co.uk
Imogen Skirving

12 rooms
£90 to £185 per room per night
Dinner from £27.50

Open all year

From the M1 (J21A): follow the A46 (Newark) for 23 miles until you reach traffic lights with garage on the corner. Turn left for Cropwell Bishop and Langar.

It's positively bucolic here. Sheep graze contentedly in front of this historic 1837 ochre building set in the unspoilt Vale of Belvoir and graced by an avenue of lime trees. There's even a pretty little Norman church to the rear; appealing, no? The look is country house smart, but relax, it's far from stuffy. There's good Georgian and Regency furniture, pretty chintz, Persian rugs and tasteful family portraits filling three reception rooms, plus an elegant neo-classical and pillared dining room. Food is a proud feature emphasising quality local ingredients and meats. Lamb and pork are reared on or next to the estate; game is shot here and roaming hens provide the freshest eggs. Chef Toby's imaginative menu changes daily; there are delicious home-made bread and jams, and superb local Stiltons. Owner Imogen Skirving has applied a nicely feminine touch to the peaceful bedrooms, all with views. The occasional ring of bells reassures guests that all's well with the world.

Love time   Dreamers and lovers flock to the Edwards room, while the Bohemia room has an imposing four-poster, real fireplace and love poetry inscribed in the bathroom. And Agnews is a very private chalet on the croquet lawn.

Love bites   Classic English country with a twist, utilising excellent local produce. Try meltingly sweet chargrilled Langar lamb, delicately flavoured poached turbot and wicked puds.

Love it up   Tour ancient Belvoir Castle, or jump to it at the nearby parachute school.

Who loves?   Designer Paul Smith is a regular.

You'll love   The picture-perfect Englishness of it all.

COTSWOLDS

Go for Ye Olde England
Eat buttered crumpets, toasted teacakes
Take a picnic hamper and champers
Bedtime story? Laurie Lee: *Cider with Rosie*

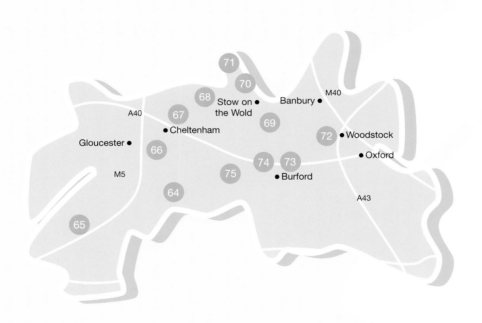

Pages 64-75

The Close Hotel

Tetbury, Gloucestershire GL8 8AQ
T 01666 502272
F 01666 504401
E 6429@greenking.co.uk
W www.theclose-hotel.com
Sarah Armriding

15 rooms
£120 to £210 per room per night
Dinner from £28.50

Open all year

From the M4 (J18): take the A46 then A433 (towards Cirencester) into Tetbury. The hotel is in the town centre.

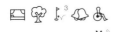

We'd say the Close – snug in the midst of the picture-book Cotswolds – is something of a heart stealer. Built in local honey-coloured stone with gables and mullioned windows, it dates back to 1596. The frontage faces the street while rooms at the rear look over a charming walled garden with a bubbling fountain. It's certainly pukka. Antiques, heavy chintz drapes and smart soft furnishings grace reception rooms, while Hepplewhite chairs, gilded mirrors and an Adams ceiling make the cream-walled dining room a class act. There's a view onto the garden, and a terrace for summer G&Ts. Menus feature ingredients raided from Gloucestershire's fertile larders (which include Prince Charles's up the road). Bedrooms also enjoy royal appointments, with handsome furnishings, fluffy robes and teddies, and well stocked hand-painted bathrooms. If you haven't yet tied the knot the Close can take care of that too, with some style.

Love time Time to get closer… so pick a richly decorated four-poster bedroom with great views over the walled gardens.
Love bites Well dressed tables grace the Cotswold-smart restaurant. Start with ravioli of blue cheese with braised celery and walnut vinaigrette, perhaps, followed by pan-fried John Dory with oyster beignets and garlic mash, then heavenly rhubarb crumble soufflé to round off.
Love it up Trawl through Tetbury's antique shops, check out Sudeley and Berkeley castles, hit some walking trails or sink a pint in a pretty pub or two.
Who loves? The Cotswold 4x4 set. Royals, too.

You'll love A place to get up Close and personal.

Thornbury Castle

Thornbury, nr. Bristol
South Gloucestershire BS35 1HH
T 01454 281182
F 01454 416188
E info@thornburycastle.co.uk
W www.thornburycastle.co.uk
Brian Jarvis

25 rooms
£130 to £370 per room per night
Dinner from £40

Open all year

From the M4 (J20): take the M5 and leave immediately at J16. Take the A38 North, then the B4061 to Thornbury, following the brown Historic Castle signs.

Castles in the air? Why bother, when Thornbury delivers such magnificent earthly pleasures. This Tudor castle-palace has significant royal antecedents: Henry VIII stayed with Ann Boleyn and his daughter Mary Tudor lived here. It's just as you might imagine, and then some. Outside it's castellated, all thick stone walls, flagged courtyards and towers. There are manicured lawns with parterres and England's oldest Tudor garden, plus a vineyard which produces the castle's own wine. Now go inside for a taste of grand oak furniture, panelling, chandeliers, tapestries, Old Masters and vast fireplaces. Bedrooms? No, these are bedchambers – with enough space for a bevy of courtiers. One canopied four-poster even lights up at the flick of a switch with moons and stars. Dining here is akin to banqueting, though on a more intimate scale. Careful restoration has preserved all the good things of the past, and matched them with the best of 21st century comforts. This is the place for sumptuous living, with staff on hand to cosset you around the clock.

Love time   Bedchambers are luxurious, characterful and honeymoon heaven.
Love bites   Three panelled dining rooms (one is in an octagonal tower) hold tables formally laid for English inspired modern cuisine. There's roast beef of Olde England on Sundays, and the signature treacle tart is wicked.
Love it up   Stroll through the Castle's splendid ten acres, take a hot-air balloon ride, play golf or explore the Cotswolds on your doorstep.
Who loves?   Kings, mistresses and well-heeled weekenders.

You'll love ❥ A place to lose your head all right (as Ann Boleyn might vouch).

The Bear of Rodborough

Rodborough Common, Stroud
Gloucestershire, GL5 5DE
T 01453 878522
F 01453 872523
E info@bearofrodborough.info
W www.cotswold-inns-hotels.co.uk
Cotswold Inns & Hotels Ltd

46 rooms
£120 to £195 per room per night
Dinner from £28.95

Open all year

From the M5 (J13): take the A419,
signed Stroud, then the A46 for
Bath/M4. Take the fourth left up hill to
Rodborough Common. From the M4:
use J18/A46 for Stroud. After
18 miles turn right for Common.

If you fancy running away in search of romance and excitement then you'll need a sense of adventure, a toothbrush and, ideally, a keen idea of where to find an old coaching inn in around 300 acres of wild countryside. The Bear of Rodborough should fit the bill nicely. The stone archway of the old tavern – with its original bell for summoning an ostler – give this hideaway, high above Stroud on the wilds of Rodborough Common, just the right vibe for welcoming the windswept in search of creature comforts. The grand old grandfather clock in the hall, fabrics, furnishings and essential good taste of the arts and crafts movement add the necessary air of simple appreciation for those who like their luxury unsmothered, and the old windows offer great views out over Woodchester Valley. Bedrooms have queen-sized beds, half-testers for those who like just a hint of the Gothic with their 1930s William Morris-style decor, and modems for those who can't wait to let the outside world know that they've run away.

Love time Draw the drapes right around the four-poster bed in Room 26.
Love bites Join the regulars for a drink at the Grizzly Bear bar and sample the best beers for miles around. The Box Tree restaurant, with its beamed ceiling and windows looking out onto the valley, is a great spot for lingering over lunch and dinner and savouring excellent roasts and fish dishes.
Love it up Tramp across the common or trawl for antiques in Cotswold villages.
Who loves? Adventurers and divas alike. Yachtsman Sir Chay Blythe sometimes dines and singer Sade is said to adore hiding away here.

You'll love ❤ The wide open spaces away from the village trail.

COTSWOLDS

Hotel on the Park

38 Evesham Road, Cheltenham
Gloucestershire, GL52 2AH
T 01242 518898
F 01242 511526
E stay@hotelonthepark.com
W www.hotelonthepark.com
Darryl & Joanne Gregory

12 rooms
£112 to £162 per room per night
Dinner from £25

Open all year

From the M5: exit at J11 (from North)
or J10 (from South) for Cheltenham, then
take the A435 (signed Evesham) from
town centre. The hotel is on the left,
opposite Pittville Park.

It's rather like staying at a private gentleman's club at Hotel on the Park, except that ladies are more than welcome too. Inside this handsome Regency villa there's a gentle hush but none of the stuffiness that often goes with it. Classically furnished with a bold, contemporary twist, you'll find dramatically draped windows, striking colour schemes and all the grandeur you'd associate with a period residence. But it's the attention to detail that makes this hotel special. We're talking mounds of fluffy hand towels, newspapers hung on poles, board games for lazy afternoons by the fire, a collection of teddy bears, a secluded courtyard garden and an array of swish and imaginative bedrooms. All 12 are done out in an eye-catching mix of Bedouin stripes, Regency cornices, Egyptian linens and Queen Anne furniture. Exotic? Very. You can soak up the splendour from free-standing bathtubs, sink into fabulous four-posters or turn the heat up in the private aromatherapy steam room in the William Clifford suite. All rooms have DVD players complete with a choice of late-night albums. And a Bedtime Bear is there for company should your darling decide to throw a huff.

Love time	Book Joseph Pitt, with its massaging bed and jacuzzi bath. Mmmm.
Love bites	Classic columns, a chequerboard floor, trompe l'oeil murals and statuary set the scene for contemporary British fare in the Bacchanalian restaurant.
Love it up	Have a flutter at Cheltenham races, mellow out in nearby Cotswold villages or step back a few centuries at Warwick Castle.
Who loves?	Kenneth Branagh and Alan Rickman park themselves here while filming.
You'll love	A Regency extravaganza where wicked weekends are positively encouraged.

The Broadway Hotel

The Green, Broadway
Worcestershire, WR12 7AA
T 01386 852401
F 01386 853879
E info@broadwayhotel.info
W www.cotswold-inns-hotels.co.uk
Cotswold Inns & Hotels Ltd

20 rooms
£130 to £150 per room per night
Dinner from £23.95

Open all year

From the M5 (J6): take the A44.
Once past Evesham,
follow signs to Broadway.
From the M40 (J8):
take the A40 to A44. Follow signs
to Evesham and Broadway.

Relive the age of Elizabeth and Essex and all those Errol Flynn-style big screen heroes amid the fabulous Tudor timbers of the Broadway Hotel in this famous corner of the Cotswolds. Of course in Good Queen Bess's day, bedrooms did not sport contemporary designer touches and almost provençal-style fabrics and colours to set off antique chests with ornate brass handles and crisp white linens. Great cartwheel chandeliers hang from the high ceilings in the lounge and dining room, and the roaring fire sets off the tone and texture of the old honey stone walls behind comfy sinkable armchairs. Once upon a time, the abbots of Pershore chose this place as a summer retreat, but today's guests are more self indulgent, whether propping up the bar, forgetting to count the calories at teatime in the lounge or remembering to draw the curtains against the mullioned windows in the bedroom.

Love time Blow out the candles at your window before sinking into a half-canopied bed.

Love bites The markets and farms of the Vale of Evesham inspire the chef and fresh flowers from Cotswolds gardens adorn the tables in the Courtyard Restaurant, with its ebony minstrels' gallery and wooden beams.

Love it up You're right at the heart of England's largest designated Area of Outstanding Natural Beauty here. Explore the gardens of nearby Hidcote Manor after rummaging in scores of antique shops.

Who loves? With Cheltenham racecourse just a gallop away, this is a hit among those whose successful flutters at the track can set hearts a-flutter at night.

You'll love A picture-book English village affair.

COTSWOLDS

The Manor House Hotel

High Street, Moreton-in-Marsh
Gloucestershire, GL56 0LJ
T 01608 650501
F 01608 651481
E info@manorhousehotel.info
W www.cotswold-inns-hotels.co.uk
Cotswold Inns & Hotels Ltd

36 rooms, 2 suites
£135 to £210 per room per night
Dinner from £29.95

Open all year

From the M40 (J8): take the A40/A44.
From the M5 (J9): take A46/A44 to
Evesham and Moreton-in-Marsh. Turn
right on to A429 for 500 yards.

The staff won't tell you who has stayed here with whom. This may be discretion or it may simply be that, thanks to this 16th century manor house's network of secret passages, they simply don't know. Given by Henry VIII to the Dean and Chapter of Westminster, the Manor House boasts a priest's hole and hidden pathways within the old stone walls – a building used to keeping its own counsel. The ivy-covered house has been restored with crafty good taste: a hint of exposed brickwork here, a vast mellow stone fireplace against fabulous wallpaper there; dark wooden bedsteads and tapestry benches in one room, more minimalist modern furnishings in another. In the bar and lounges, huge copper bedwarmers hang beside a log fire whose yellow stones are blackened by centuries of winter fires. In the bathrooms, discover Molton Brown gels and lotions for private pampering.

Love time   Climb the steps up into the fairytale four-poster in Room Eight.
Love bites   The Mulberry bar and restaurant – voted Cotswold Restaurant of the Year in 2004 – is renowned for its seasonal menus: taste the mulberries in cocktails, sauces and desserts. Indulge in prime Scottish beef cooked in red wine and shallots, or confit of duck leg partnered with a wild mushroom cassoulet.
Love it up   Moreton-in-Marsh is the gateway to the Evenlode Valley, and an easy drive to Sudeley castle – home to Liz Hurley's pal Henry Dent-Brocklehurst.
Who loves?   Royalty have been known to drop in here for tea.

You'll love ▶ Rambling Cotswold manor house steeped in history.

The Noel Arms

High Street, Chipping Campden
Gloucestershire GL55 6AT
T 01386 840317
F 01386 841136
E reception@noelarmshotel.com
W www.noelarmshotel.com
Christa & Ian Taylor

27 rooms
£125 to £195 per room per night
Dinner from £30 à la carte

Open all year

From the A40: take the A424 through
Burford and past Stow on the Wold to
join A44. Turn right onto the
B4081 for Chipping Campden. The
hotel faces the village square.

Sweeter than a box of Milk Tray, Chipping Campden is the kind of place that keeps lovebirds flocking to the Cotswolds, and the Noel Arms is yet another excellent reason to pay a visit. New owners Ian and Christa Taylor have been pampering guests at Cotswold House across the street for years, and have recently spread their wings to embrace this village favourite as well. Its golden Cotswold stone exterior, dark wooden beams, cosy fireplaces and fresh flowers are a recipe for romance, and the air of unpretentious comfort will quickly make you feel at home. Charles II sought refuge from the Roundheads here in 1651, and lovers on the run from the pressures of modern life can be sure of sanctuary today. So get glammed up for dinner, chat over a pint in the Drover's bar, put your feet up in the lounge or head out to explore the village – whatever lights your fire is here.

Love time Snuggle up in a carved four-poster that dates back to 1657.
Love bites Treat yourself to a touch of the exotic: head chef Peter Xu prepares delicious Chinese, Japanese, Malaysian and Thai dishes, interspersed with traditional European fare. Or pop over the road to sister hotel Cotswold House, where you can dine in elegance in Juliana's Restaurant, or relax in lively Hick's Brasserie.
Love it up Shop till you drop in Chipping Campden's irresistible galleries, or lace up your boots for an invigorating hike on the Cotswold Way.
Who loves? The Campden set – they've been coming here for years.

You'll love ➤ Oodles of character at the heart of Shakespeare country.

Cotswold House

The Square, Chipping Campden
Gloucestershire, GL55 6AN
T 01386 840330
F 01386 840310
E reception@cotswoldhouse.com
W www.cotswoldhouse.com
Christa & Ian Taylor

21 rooms
£205 to £650 per room per night
Dinner from £45

Open all year

From the A40: take the A424 through Burford and past Stow on the Wold to join A44. Turn right onto the B4081 for Chipping Campden. The hotel is on the village square.

The ravishing village of Chipping Campden (rated England's prettiest by those in the know) is home to Cotswold House, a graceful Regency hotel built of honey-coloured Cotswold stone, with a soaring spiral staircase that's pure Jane Austen. But prepare for some surprises: this olde-worlde facade hides some ultra-chic contemporary interiors. Gadget junkies will be in heaven here – bedrooms are equipped with state-of-the-art technology. There are Bang & Olufsen entertainment systems, ISDN lines, and even plasma TV screens in the bathrooms, so you can soak blissfully while watching your favourite soap. Uncluttered rooms are done up in chic shades of slate, plum and purple, with huge beds and sloping ceilings. Planning to spend your entire stay under cover? Then you'll want to study the bespoke bedding menu, which lets you choose from a range of pillows, cashmere blankets and Frette linen sheets. Should you surface, the Bellinis at the bar downstairs are the best outside Venice.

Love time   Try one of the ultra-chic Cottage suites; one even has a garden with its own private outdoor hot tub.
Love bites   Slip into something chic and drift to your table at Juliana's restaurant, where delicacies like Orkney scallops served with truffled cabbage, mussel cream and lemon confit grace the menu. Or head for vibey Hick's Brasserie, where you can order anything from tempura to burgers.
Love it up   Browse in Chipping Campden's gift shops for some rural retail therapy.
Who loves?   The Old Grammar School suite is a fave with rock stars.

You'll love   High technology and contemporary chic in a chocolate-box village.

The Feathers

Market Street, Woodstock
Oxfordshire OX20 1SX
T 01993 812291
F 01993 813158
E enquiries@feathers.co.uk
W www.feathers.co.uk
Jeremy du Plessis

15 rooms, 5 suites
£135 to £225 per room per night
Dinner from £39

Open all year

From the M40 (J9):
take the A34 to Oxford and A44 to
Woodstock and Blenheim Palace.
Turn left after the traffic lights in
Woodstock.

This palpably pretty hotel could melt any heart into submission. Its location, in one of England's famously lovely country towns – all ancient buildings and mellow Cotswold stone – provides an "ooh-aah" setting for the Feathers itself, with its tumbling window boxes and pretty walled courtyard garden. Seven buildings, dating back to the 17th century, have been artfully and stylishly combined, while labyrinthine passageways and tiny stairs underline the olde-worlde charm. Classic English country house style is pepped up with contemporary decorative twists, in soft and restful colours. Bedrooms are high on luxury and baths are indulgent. Nowadays there's even more pampering, courtesy of Preen, the hotel's new beauty and body treatment spa, where you can relax with a back rub (unless your beloved obliges), before enjoying the chef's award-winning cuisine. You'll be tickled at the Feathers when Johann, the parrot, squawks a friendly greeting – and should you arrive feeling tired and ruffled, obliging staff make this just the place to smooth things out.

Love time
The temperature's rising in the Goldcrest suite (is it you or your own private steamroom?), while the Junior suite has a little garden terrace.

Love bites
Salivate over tender roast rump of lamb with goat's cheese ravioli in the antique-panelled restaurant, or spear tiger prawn brochettes in the bar.

Love it up
Check out magnificent Blenheim Palace (Churchill's birthplace) and Oxford's dreaming spires – or try quadbiking, chauffeured punting and ballooning.

Who loves?
Guests include Gwyneth Paltrow, Johnny Depp and John Malkovich.

You'll love
Being pampered in Preen – it's holistic heaven.

COTSWOLDS

Burford House

99 High Street, Burford
Oxfordshire, OX18 4QA
T 01993 823151
F 01993 823240
E stay@burfordhouse.co.uk
W www.burfordhouse.co.uk
Jane & Simon Henty

7 rooms, 1 suite
£110 to £155 per room per night

Closed Christmas and two weeks Jan

From London: take the M40/A40 direct to Burford. Turn right at the roundabout for the High Street.

Small but perfectly formed, this Tudor house with its low ceilings, leaded windows, old beams and log fires stands proud in a pretty Cotswold town bursting with antique shops and tea rooms. But there's nothing twee about these luxury lodgings, whose rooms are ravishingly styled with a mix of old oak furniture, books, family pictures and porcelain. Shiny bathrooms are designed for spending time in, with roll-top tubs, power showers and an array of bubbles positively encouraging steamy goings-on. There are only eight bedrooms here, so breakfast is an informal rather than a starchy affair and it's well worth staying in for the evening, when the honesty bar – stocked with terrific home-made damson gin, quince vodka and a dozen malt whiskies – comes into its own. But it's the hands-on touch and attention to detail of hosts Jane and Simon Henty that makes this stylish abode so special, with hand-written menus, a resident cat, vases of fresh flowers and classical music creating a relaxed sense of ease. If you can tear yourselves away from the bedrooms, the garden outside is awash with flowers.

Love time   Expect Tudor-style four-posters and marble bathrooms. We loved Sherbourne, with its tub for two.

Love bites   Think freshly-baked granary bread and delicious home-made cakes, locally smoked salmon and aged farmhouse cheeses. A feast of local fare is served up for hearty breakfasts, light lunches and wicked teas.

Love it up   Trawl for antiques in the High Street or head to Oxford for some punting.

Who loves?   Suitors poised to pop the question: betrothals are rife here!

You'll love ❥   Rustic beams, creaking floors and a nicely fuzzy echo of times past.

The Bay Tree Hotel

Sheep Street, Burford
Oxfordshire, OX18 4LW
T 01993 822791
F 01993 823008
E info@baytreehotel.info
W www.cotswold-inns-hotels.co.uk
Cotswold Inns & Hotels

14 rooms, 7 suites
£165 to £240 per room per night
Dinner from £28.95

Open all year

From the M40 (J8) or M5 (J11):
follow the A40 to Burford.
From the M4 (J15): follow
the A419/A361 to Burford.
From the High Street turn into
Sheep Street.

There's nothing lightweight or flimsy about this Bay Tree – it positively groans with history and a sense of occasion. Centuries-old Cotswold stone walls, substantial drapes, heavy oak doors and a well trodden wooden staircase lead to opulently furnished bedrooms. The high wooden beds, covered with rich quilted spreads, are veritable occasions in their own right, in rooms where bedtime is a ritual to be savoured. Classic ground-floor rooms look out onto a walled rose and herb garden, with the heady scent wafting in through open windows in summer. A keen modern hand mixes the antiques and grand tapestries so that the feel remains country house and not museum. In winter, relax by a lazy log fire after exploring the quaint market town of Burford. In summer, sit on the terrace sipping a Pimms as you count the butterflies and plan a drive out to Blenheim Palace.

Love time The Oak master suite is a leap through centuries of luxury, a weekend in its own right. Lap up the four-poster, lavish lounge and whirling jacuzzi.

Love bites Cosy up by the ingleook fireplace in the oak-panelled Woolsack bar, then step into the award-winning restaurant whose candles are reflected in polished window panes overlooking the rose garden. Old flagstone floors and antique dressers contrast with cutting-edge British cuisine celebrating the best of local produce. Don't miss the lavish Cotswold teas either.

Love it up Discover Oxford's dreaming spires or the million photo opportunities of the Cotswolds, right on the doorstep.

Who loves? Ruby Wax and David Furnish have both checked in.

You'll love ⤷ The grand gesture of it all.

The Swan at Bibury

Bibury, Gloucestershire, GL7 5NW
T 01285 740695
F 01285 740473
E info@swanhotel.co.uk
W www.cotswold-inns-hotels.co.uk
Cotswold Inns & Hotels Ltd

18 rooms
£140 to £260 per room per night
Dinner from £29.95

Open all year

From the M4 (J15): take the A419 and B4425 to Cirencester and Bibury. From the M40/A40: follow road to Burford, then B4425 to Bibury. From the M5 (J11A) take A417 to Cirencester, then B4425 to Bibury.

There are Cotswolds and there are Cotswolds, and Bibury is about as Cotswold as you can get. William Morris, who knew a thing or two about style, declared this spot the prettiest village in England. With its ivy-covered golden stone walls and views of the River Coln's weeping willows, the Swan instantly recreates the mood of a timeless England. Walk in through the front door and pass a baby grand, revel in the eclectic decor – a Mackintosh chair or watercolour here, an Art Deco mirror there – and know that your bedroom will have just that 1920s lost weekend feel. Perhaps a vintage Roberts radio to set the musical mood to an era before hi-fi, possibly a chandelier, certainly fluffy bathrobes for two. Naturally, service is friendly and top-notch. Since the Swan is a veritable proposal in waiting, it's not surprising to find that it boasts a range of wedding suites. Best is the Swan Sanctuary, a haven for relaxation and beauty therapy.

Love time   Wallow then whirl in one of the three Deluxe rooms with a canopied bed and jacuzzi.

Love bites   High ceilings, red walls and tall windows in the Signet room set the scene here for Grant Tompkins' award-winning contemporary British cuisine. He tickles fresh Bibury trout into a mouthwatering dish and changes dinner menus daily.

Love it up   Catch *Romeo and Juliet* at nearby Stratford-upon-Avon or plan a happy ending along the river banks.

Who loves?   Name-dropping would be terribly out of place here.

You'll love   Life on a chocolate box.

EAST ANGLIA

Go for beaches, boats and birdlife
Eat fresh Norfolk oysters
Take plenty of fizz
Bedtime story? Daniel Defoe: *Moll Flanders*

80

● Cromer

81

79

Kings Lynn ●

A47

● Peterborough

Norwich ●

● Great Yarmouth

A11

A12

Cambridge ●

78

Ipswich ●

● Felixstowe

82

83

● Colchester

● Chelmsford

● Southend-on-Sea

Pages 78-83

Sheene Mill

Station Road, Melbourn
Cambridgeshire SG8 6DX
T 01763 261393
F 01763 261376
E info@sheenemill.co.uk
W www.sheenemill.co.uk
Sally & Steven Saunders

9 rooms
£95 to £120 per room per night
Dinner from £35

Closed Boxing Day and New Year's Day

From the M11 (J11): take the A10 towards Royston. Continue past Royston to the village of Melbourn then turn left into Station Road to the hotel.

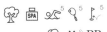

You can bed down in celebrity style at this fabulously stylish watermill on the river Mel, complete with bobbing ducks and springtime daffodils. Star rooms carry a top designer's signature. Fancy portholes, mermaid murals and a water bed? Then make waves in the Water room. Flashes of tartan? Have a highland fling in John Amabile's distinctly celtic Mcbedroom. Not-so-chaste nights under the covers? David Emanuel's virginal white boudoir should do the trick. Themed rooms apart, this timbered 17th century mill offers brilliant food, too. The owner is none other than TV chef and organic food champion Steven Saunders, who together with wife Sally delivers big time on the culinary front. The mantra is organic, using first-class seasonal British ingredients. You'll dine in the vibrant Med-style dining room with its dazzling yellow and purple colours, modern art and nightly piano jazz. The mill itself is warm and convivial (think plump sofas, log fires, friendly staff), and it's not surprisingly honeymoon heaven. Steal away here if you're already hitched or just fancy a little sinfulness far from the daily grind.

Love time   It'll be all white on the night in the virginal Honeymoon suite. We're blushing.
Love bites   Daily-written menus offer eclectic dining: try smoked salmon and Avruga caviar blini, breast of Norfolk duckling with five-spice and honey sauce, and Cointreau creme brulée.Top wines naturally – many organic.
Love it up   Dip into Cambridge and drift around in a punt, follow walking trails through green countryside, or turn chef with some one-to-one cookery lessons.
Who loves?   Watersprites and lazy weekenders.

You'll love   Culinary thrills, not run-of-the-mill, OK?

Congham Hall Country House

Grimston, nr. King's Lynn
Norfolk PE32 1AH
T 01485 600250
F 01485 601191
E info@conghamhallhotel.co.uk
W www.conghamhallhotel.co.uk
Julie Woodhouse

14 rooms
£165 to £350 per room per night
Dinner £29.50 to £36

Open all year

From the M11 (J14): take the A10 towards Ely and King's Lynn. Congham Hall is located off the A148 in Grimston, six miles from the town.

RR

The sparkle of candlelight on crystal, the distant thwack of leather on willow, sheer drapes billowing in the morning breeze and the luxurious touch of a soft bathrobe as you stand at the window looking out over a walled country garden. No wonder Norfolk's country house experience is a favourite choice of princes and princesses. Just a stone's throw from the royal family's Sandringham home is Congham Hall, a white Georgian manor house standing in gracious parkland and orchards with a well stocked kitchen garden, elegant flower beds, a chef's selection of more than 700 herbs and even its own cricket pitch. Understated elegance in the best of taste is the keynote here. Bedrooms are softly lit, and the subtle scent of potpourri and garden flowers adds a floral note. You could even arrive for your tryst in one of the hotel's private helicopters.

Love time   Try the extravagant Garden suite, where French windows open onto a country garden and champagne breakfast is de rigueur. With a bath almost as wide as the king-size bed, you might never find the great outdoors.

Love bites   The hotel's Orangery restaurant serves game from the royal estate and vegetables hand-picked from the kitchen garden. All are presented with flair and panache.

Love it up   Take a midnight stroll in the 30-acre grounds, or head for the coast and watch seals at Blakeney Point. Recreate scenes from *Shakespeare in Love* at Holkham Beach, or wander through fields of Norfolk lavender.

Who loves?   The area's most famous son, Nelson, wooed Lady Hamilton nearby.

You'll love   Gracious living amid gardens where the birds and bees make busy.

The Gin Trap Inn

6 High Street, Ringstead
Norfolk PE36 5JU
T 01485 525264
F 01485 525321
E info@gintrap.co.uk
W www.gintrapinn.co.uk
Don & Margaret Greer

3 rooms
£80 to £120 per room per night
Dinner from £22.50

Open all year

From King's Lynn: take the A149 to Heacham. Turn right and follow the signs for Ringstead. You can't miss the Gin Trap.

This 17th century Norfolk coaching inn, complete with cosy beamed bar and crackling fire, has been welcoming weary travellers for centuries. It makes a great base from which to explore the lovely beaches and wild coastal paths of North Norfolk and has just three delightful cottage-style bedrooms, beautifully but simply done out with claw-foot baths, wonderful brass beds, scatter cushions and floral fabrics. With its window seats and shutters, low latch doors and mellow timbers, the Gin Trap oozes olde-worlde charm. Polished brass and old artefacts on the walls lend a traditional feel, while attention to detail ensures that comfort is paramount. You'll find all the atmosphere of a village inn at the bar downstairs, with hand-pumped ales and first-rate food. Cuddle up by the log fire here in winter and enjoy alfresco dining in the summer when the sunny walled garden comes into its own. You can mingle with the locals in the bar before treating yourselves to farm-fresh dishes, impeccably presented from a lively menu.

Love time   Take Room One, with its chandelier, Victorian brass bedstead and free-standing bathtub.

Love bites   Fresh locally-sourced Norfolk produce features strongly in a stylish repertoire of dishes from an award-winning chef. Local seafood is not surprisingly as fresh as it gets.

Love it up   Mosey around Ringstead's art gallery and antique emporium, visit a bird reserve, stroll on near-empty beaches or visit stately Sandringham.

Who loves?   Townies in search of village-inn tranquillity.

You'll love   Beds far too good to get out of.

Beechwood Hotel

Cromer Road, North Walsham
Norfolk NR28 0HD
T 01692 403231
F 01692 407284
E enquiries@beechwood-hotel.co.uk
W www.beechwood-hotel.co.uk
Don Birch & Lindsay Spalding

17 rooms
£90 to £170 per room per night
Dinner from £34

Closed 1 Jan – 15 Feb

From Norwich: take the B1150 to North Walsham from ring road. Turn left at first set of lights on entering the town, and right at the next. The hotel is 150 yards further on.

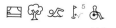

A summer stroll with the breeze ruffling drifts of sea lavender and the singing of skylarks high above your head – sounds good? Perfectly positioned for exploring North Norfolk's waterways and wild beaches, this traditional red brick Georgian country house, clad in Virginia creeper and set in a pretty garden, is a cracker. Proprietors Don Birch and Lindsay Spalding and their staff seem to have struck just the right balance between warmth and professionalism at Beechwood, winner of the Visit Britain Hotel of the Year 2003 award. No wonder the guest book here is full of rave reviews. Arriving guests are welcomed with afternoon tea and the comfortable drawing room is well stocked with books and magazines. Pre-dinner drinks are served in the flower-filled garden on summer evenings. Spacious bedrooms are furnished with period Victorian furniture, while CD players, Molton Brown smellies and fluffy bathrobes add up-to-the-minute cosseting touches.

Love time   Come up and see me sometime… in a Mae West style slipper bath or four-poster bed hand-made in Norfolk – features of the airy Garden rooms.

Love bites   Cromer crab, Morston mussels and Sheringham lobster all feature regularly in award-winning chef Steven Norgate's fabulous Ten Mile Dinner – where as many ingredients as possible are sourced within some ten miles of the hotel. Has to be worth travelling miles for.

Love it up   With royalty at Sandringham, birds at the coastal reserves and nature lovers on North Norfolk's marshland and beaches.

Who loves?   This was once Agatha Christie's Norfolk hideaway.

You'll love   An impeccable bedside manner.

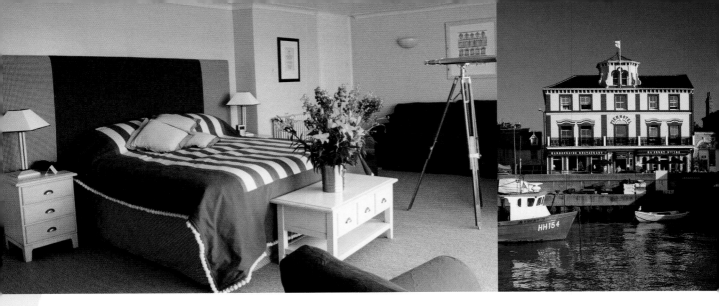

The Pier at Harwich

The Quay, Harwich
Essex CO12 3HH
T 01255 241212
F 01255 551922
E pier@milsomhotels.com
W www.milsomhotels.com
Gerald & Paul Milsom

14 rooms
£95 to £170 per room per night
Dinner from £30

Open all year

From the A12: take the A120 for
Harwich, north of Colchester.
The Pier Hotel is a short distance from
the rail station and is also accessible
by boat.

You're bang on the quayside of Harwich's historic port here, where packet ships once set sail for Europe. The steamships of old have now been replaced by speedy car ferries, making the Pier the perfect base for channel-hoppers seeking a pre- or post-voyage sojourn. You might even decide to ditch your deck shoes, pull down the hatches and enjoy an extended stay here instead. Landlubbers will like the decor's restful sand, sea and stone tones, heightened by nautical accents. Public rooms have a pleasing buzz (perfect for the two of you to splice the mainbrace perhaps), while senior and junior ranking staff have evidently been signed up for good service. This is a great seafarer's town, so take a deep breath of the briny and watch yachts and cruise liners chug by, or take in a bird's eye view over the estuary from your bedroom window. This is oyster country, so it could be just the place to drop anchor and uncork the champers.

Love time   Try the king-size comfort of the Mayflower suite. There's even a telescope for you to play I-Spy.

Love bites   The Pier's prize-winning Harbourside restaurant and informal Ha'Penny Bistro major on seafood (delivered fresh from the quayside each morning), so tuck into catch of the day.

Love it up   Follow a bracing walk along the waterfront with a mooch into Harwich, birthplace of Captain Jones, who sailed the Mayflower to the New World. Historic Colchester is an easy drive from here.

Who loves?   Landlubbers who enjoy sailing into a safe haven.

You'll love   Sea-bright views and sea-fresh food.

EAST ANGLIA

Maison Talbooth

Stratford Road, Dedham
Colchester, Essex CO7 6HN
T 01206 322367
F 01206 322752
E maison@milsomhotels.com
W www.milsomhotels.com
Gerald & Paul Milsom

10 rooms
£165 to £275 per room per night
Dinner from £40

Open all year

From the M25 (J28): take the A12 past Colchester towards Ipswich Take the slip road signed Dedham/Stratford St Mary and after a mile turn right onto the Stratford Road. The hotel is half a mile further on.

Impeccable good taste is the order of the day at this handsome former Victorian rectory. Father and son team Gerald and Paul Milsom, whose flair has helped win the Maison international acclaim, provide a winning formula of elegant accommodation and top-notch cuisine. The hotel is superbly positioned on a bluff overlooking the Stour river valley, with green fields stretching out to the medieval church at Stratford St Mary. This sylvan setting has inspired many a would-be Constable (whose famous painting of Dedham Vale captured the building that is now Le Talbooth restaurant) to reach for their brushes. Bedrooms are now undergoing serious re-fits, with dazzling new cool and contemporary suites – all granite, glass and free-standing baths – sitting alongside more traditional guest quarters. And there's no need to emerge from under the duvet here – breakfast is brought to you in bed.

Love time   Splash out in the circular whirlpool bath in Keats, or soak beneath the power showers of up-to-the-minute Browning and Shelley.

Love bites   Dining is taken seriously at Le Talbooth, where diners gaze out at ducks bobbing on the water amid trailing willows. Inside the beamed dining room, with its chic upholstery, expect award-winning food and spot-on service. Try the chateaubriand, and perhaps round off your meal with a titillating gypsy tart…

Love it up   Play giant chess on the lawn or trawl for antiques in nearby villages.

Who loves?   Townies who feel totally at home à la Maison.

You'll love ❥   A taste of country life barely an hour from London.

SOUTH

Go for the season's top sporting dates
Eat pass the canapés, darling
Take plenty of bling
Bedtime story? Jilly Cooper: *Polo*

Pages 86-95

Langtry Manor

Derby Road, East Cliff
Bournemouth, Dorset BH1 3QB
T 01202 553887
F 01202 290115
E lillie@langtrymanor.co.uk
W www.langtrymanor.co.uk
The Howard family

15 rooms, 5 suites
£158 to £238 per room per night
Dinner from £29

Closed 3-13 Jan

From London: take M3, M27, A31 and A338 to Bournemouth. Take first exit at the first roundabout (St Paul's), and go straight over the next. Take first left into Knyveton Road. Langtry Manor is at the corner of Derby Road.

Built by King Edward VII for illicit assignations with his mistress Lillie Langtry in 1877, Langtry Manor still keeps faithful to its Victorian and Edwardian antecedents. The lovers' imprint is palpable here. For instance, you can see it in the warmly wood-panelled King's room, whose lofty ceiling was built to disperse regal cigar smoke. The huge carved oak fireplace has hand-painted Shakespearean tiles to reflect their mutual love of theatre; tie-back hooks have royal emblems and their initials are touchingly engraved everywhere; there's a display of memorabilia too. The splendid dining room, with its white enamelled panels, has a peephole, so that His Maj could easily view his guests before entering. An award-winning chef replicates the banqueting feasts Edward was fond of with a sumptuous six-course menu, while waiting staff are garbed in period costume. The Howard family run this kingly abode with spirit and warmth. You can pretend you're royalty here (and get away with it).

Love time The Lillie Langtry room, with its richly draped four-poster, heart-shaped jacuzzi and Romeo and Juliet balcony is made for lovers' trysts. Expect a flower on your pillow, champagne cocktails, bedside chocolate and treats.

Love bites A minstrel's gallery, stained glass windows featuring intertwined heart-shaped swans, and delicious cooking make the dining room a treat.

Love it up Explore Bournemouth and the New Forest, stroll along a prize-winning beach or keep fit with a free day pass to a top leisure centre.

Who loves? Present-day Berties and Lillies.

You'll love A lovenest built by a king – just the place to go a-wooing.

Stanwell House

14-15 High Street, Lymington
Hampshire SO41 9AA
T 01590 677123
F 01590 677756
E sales@stanwellhouse.co.uk
W www.stanwellhousehotel.co.uk
Mark Hewitt

24 rooms, 5 suites
£110 to £160 per room per night
Dinner from £25

Open all year

From M3: take M27/M271 towards
Southampton, then join the A35/A337
to Lymington. The hotel is on
the main street.

Swathes of velvets and sumptuous silks draping four-poster beds and shading the windows, a negligent negligee left on plump pillows, a half-sipped glass of champagne to one side... the bedrooms and suites in Jane McIntyre's Georgian hotel tell their own tales of stolen weekends. The rich ripe colours of indulgence mark out this very individual hotel and cottage annexe tucked away between Lymington's yacht harbour and the New Forest. Take the orthodox route through the charmingly decorated hotel, with its bare board and York stone floors, vibrant jewel shades, antique and bric-a-brac laden shelves and candlelit dining room, or role-play a romantic rendezvous in the old walled garden or a tryst on the balcony of a private suite. The spirit of Lymington's seafaring past and present imbues the cobbled streets of this pretty seaport, while fond reunions are celebrated with luscious cream teas and decadent cocktails within the hotel walls or behind locked doors.

Love time Bathrooms pamper every whim, with roll-top baths for two or invigorating power showers.

Love bites Whisper confidences or toast promises over fresh-cut flowers and fine wines in the award-winning bistro. Delicious fare here ranges from fresh catch of the day to wild boar sausages.

Love it up Let the Solent put wind in your sails or get lost in the nearby New Forest.

Who loves? Honeymooners staying at the private Elgar's cottage next door (where there's room service till late) aren't saying...

You'll love Dramatic interiors and a riot of colour twixt Hardy country and the sea.

The George Hotel

Quay Street, Yarmouth
Isle of Wight PO41 0PE
T 01983 760331
F 01983 760425
E res@thegeorge.co.uk
W www.thegeorge.co.uk
John Illsley & Jeremy Willcock

17 rooms
£180 to £245 per room per night
Brasserie dinner from £35
Restaurant dinner from £45

Closed New Year's Day

From Lymington: take the Yarmouth car ferry. The hotel is a few minutes from the harbour.

You don't have to be a yachtie to enjoy life at this imposing 17th century Yarmouth townhouse on the water's edge. Landlubbers will like the fact that it doesn't overdo the nautical theme. There's lots of elegant panelling, period furniture, a stone-flagged entrance and a merry log fire, while the garden and terrace with tables overlooking the Solent are ideal for splicing the mainbrace in good weather. Sea breezes tend to whip up appetites and chef Kevin Mangeolles (three AA rosettes) understands how to satiate them with modern British cuisine using French influences. The informal yellow brasserie is just the place to tuck into fresh sea bass with crab ravioli, while the lavish George restaurant is the place for dinner, delivering serious modern British and internationally influenced cuisine. Try turbot flavoured with "spice of angels" perhaps, or Bresse chicken. Drop anchor in deeply comfortable rooms – some with balconies and views – or splash around in good sized baths. The sound of water gently lapping outside certainly floats our boat.

Love time	Rooms with antique pine panelling vie with those in green, blue or lilac. Another is done out in rich autumn shades with an oak four-poster.
Love bites	Excellent fish and organic produce feature among the day-long temptations on offer here from an accomplished chef.
Love it up	Go sailing, or charter Master George, the hotel boat, for the day. Explore historic Yarmouth and the island's cute Enid Blyton villages, or hit the beach.
Who loves?	Weekend sailors and those who can't resist being on the water.

You'll love ❤ By George! All comes right on the Isle of Wight.

SOUTH

Priory Bay

Priory Drive, Seaview
Isle of Wight PO34 5BU
T 01983 613146
F 01983 616539
E enquiries@priorybay.co.uk
W www.priorybay.co.uk
Andrew Palmer

18 rooms
£120 to £280 per room per night
Dinner from £27.50

Open all year

From Portsmouth: take the ferry to Fishbourne. Join the A3055 to Sandown, turn left onto the B3330 for Bembridge and then left towards Seaview.

This characterful country house by the sea started life as a medieval priory. It's also been a Tudor farmhouse and home to Georgian gentry. These palpable layers of history add to the appeal of Priory Bay, with its commanding views over the Solent. Surrounded by 70 rolling acres and sitting atop its own private beach, this is a place to tarry awhile. Tastefully furnished lounges have high ceilings, plump sofas, huge sash windows and period touches. Giant murals of old-time Bembridge – now the island's trendiest seaside resort – line the restaurant walls, and there's plenty of alfresco terrace dining in summer. You can claw your way through juicy lobsters at the Oyster Bar in the woods above the bay before exploring the sandy shore and rock pools below. Bedrooms – all individual – range from cottagey to classic, with the finest being in the main house. For the coolest arrival, ask the hotel's private launch to collect you in Portsmouth and land you on the beach. You'll have sand between your toes before you've even checked in.

Love time Pick the bedroom that's for you: beamed and nautical with timbered walls; floral and antique-strewn; or smart Edwardian with a clawfoot bath.

Love bites Seared scallops, skate wing on a fricassee of wild mushrooms, roasted saddle of venison and quince and cranberry crumble are highlights of an eclectic modern European menu.

Love it up Get the wind in your hair with great sailing and watersports. Golf, tennis, an outdoor pool and your own beach are right on the doorstep.

Who loves? The Island set – regulars come back here year after year.

You'll love ❥ A slice of the Isle of Wight where everything's just right.

Esseborne Manor

Hurstbourne Tarrant, Andover
Hampshire SP11 0ER
T 01264 736444
F 01264 736725
E info@esseborne-manor.co.uk
W www.essebornemanor.com
Ian & Lucilla Hamilton

15 rooms
£120 to £180 per room per night
Dinner from £30

Open all year

From the M4 (J13): take the A34
South and turn off at the
A343 (marked Highclere)
towards Andover.
Esseborne is 1.5 miles north of the
village of Hurstbourne Tarrant.

Rolling meadows, acres of farmland and sheep grazing on the north Wessex downs; the click-clack of croquet on the lawn and the tinkle of ice in tall summer glasses of Pimms: sometimes true luxury is to be found outside the windows. A firm favourite with lovers of the English outdoors, Ian and Lucilla Hamilton's manor house has been a country retreat for more than a century and offers a tantalising taste of time-out as enjoyed by the privileged classes. If you fancy a pagan rite or two at nearby Stonehenge, an illicit moment of passion in the Bourne Valley countryside, or an afternoon wrapped in fluffy robes under the silk drapes of the Madingly room's four-poster, feel free. You can always be respectable later on when you take tea overlooking the grounds or dither over the menu in front of the log fire in the dining room.

Love time For a very private party for two, choose the Ferndown room. A spa bath and secluded patio make the most of indoor and outdoor moments.

Love bites Inspired by an array of herbs from the garden and the varied tastes of an A-list clientele, chef David rustles up duck with kumquats, gnocchi with truffles and parmesan, and even chocolate and thyme soup for dessert.

Love it up Live it up here, feeling the wind in your hair as you drive your convertible through thatched villages, wallowing in a nearby health spa or just tramping through the open countryside.

Who loves? Royal weekenders, government ministers and country gentry. The guest list would read like *Who's Who* – but that's not for publication.

You'll love The essence of Englishness.

The Brocket Arms

Ayot St Lawrence, Welwyn
Hertfordshire AL6 9BT
T 01438 820250
F 01438 820068
W www.brocketarms.com
Toby Wingfield-Digby

6 rooms
£70 to £80 per room per night
Dinner from £21

Open all year

From the A1(M): take the B656 at J6.
Ayot St Lawrence is signed from here.

This traditional 14th century inn looks sweet as pie with its leaded windows, leaning walls and criss-cross beams in the pretty Hertfordshire village of Ayot St Lawrence. In good weather there's a sun-trapping walled garden, and when chills set in there's a vast inglenook fireplace. Ceilings are low, oak staves are everywhere and walls are adorned with local watercolours. This place has quite a history: prior to the Reformation it was the monastic quarters for the Norman church. A friendly ghost has been sighted in the bar area, but so far he hasn't made it upstairs to the six rooms where all is comfy and cosy. Anticipate honest English cooking in a dining room with more duck-your-head (or grouse!) beams and quarry tiled floors. Lunch might find you tucking into a home-made steak pie or rare roast beef. Candlelit dinner might feature roast pheasant, grilled sea bass or Mediterranean prawns. Needless to say there are good ales (and wines too), and if you're collared by one of the friendly regulars, lots of good tales. Mine hosts are Toby and Deirdre Wingfield-Digby, who provide the jollity that characterises the Brocket.

Love time Bag the made-for-nookie four-poster Honeymoon suite up in the eaves.
Love bites Beams, stone floors and candlelight set the scene for game and home-cooked traditional fare.
Love it up Go for bracing country walks, or visit Shaw's Corner, home of playwright George Bernard Shaw; imposing Hatfield House and Knebworth; and the street markets of cathedral city St Albans.
Who loves? Londoners after some country living on the doorstep.

You'll love Being snug as a bug in a time-warp.

Eastwell Manor

Eastwell Park, Boughton Lees
Ashford, Kent TN25 4HR
T 01233 213000
F 01233 635530
E enquiries@eastwellmanor.co.uk
W www.eastwellmanor.co.uk
The Parrett family

62 rooms
£140 to £395 per room per night
Dinner from £37.50

Open all year

From the M20 (J9): take the A28 direct to Boughton Lees. From the M2 (J6): take the A251 to join the A28. By Eurostar: Ashford International is ten minutes from the hotel.

Surrounded by glorious Kent countryside (think bluebell woods, apple orchards and cricket on the village green – it doesn't get much more bucolic than this), this grand country manor will inspire you to exercise a spot of droit de seigneur. It's an imposing, ivy-clad ancestral home, complete with gables, turrets, fountains and 3,000 acres of grounds. In short, Eastwell has all the ingredients needed for a romantic liaison in grand style – just add you. Rooms have stunning views over manicured lawns or rolling countryside. The Pavilion spa is an extravagance of sleek furnishings, floral fabrics and trompe l'oeil murals where heavenly treatments are the order of the day – take pampering to the max with a caviar facial or body treatment in the Dreams beauty salon. Ensconce yourself within the walls of the original house or seek seclusion in one of the mews cottages, where you can turn cook for the night or order in a banquet from the kitchens.

Love time   Choose one of the Manor rooms for sprawling four-postered splendour.
Love bites   Guests dine on impeccable Franco-British cuisine and choose from a weighty wine list in the opulent cream and amber restaurant. Fancy something less formal? The Brasserie in the Pavilion serves delicious lighter fare.
Love it up   Make a pilgrimage to historic Canterbury (after a few pleasurable sins the night before), or hop on Eurostar for a continental crusade.
Who loves?   Queen Victoria and Prince Albert spent many nights of conjugal bliss here. So may you.

You'll love ❯ Grand style in the Garden of England.

Wallett's Court Country House

Westcliffe, St Margaret's Bay
Dover, Kent CT15 6EW
T 01304 852424
F 01304 853430
E stay@wallettscourt.com
W www.wallettscourt.com

13 rooms, 4 suites
£119 to £159 per room per night
Dinner from £35

Closed 24-26 Dec

From the M2 or M20: take the A258 to Deal, then the first right to St-Margaret's-at-Cliffe and follow the road for another mile.

Here's the perfect overnight roost en route to the Continent – though it's a shame not to dawdle at Wallett's Court, a characterful 17th century Kentish manor house just three miles from Dover. Saved from near-dereliction 30 years ago by the Oakley family, it has been nurtured back to life in some style, and now offers a warm and welcoming base in the Kentish countryside. Baronial hearths, carved wood, exposed brickwork and wall paintings add to the sense of history, while gardens giving way to seven acres of rolling landscape pile on the charm. Bedrooms come in an array of sizes and styles – choose one that's richly four-postered in the main house, or cool and contemporary in the newer wings. Dining in the oak-beamed restaurant, with its tapestried chairs and cosy lamps, is de rigueur. Cooking is excellent, so all the more reason for a workout in the gym or a set of tennis next morning. Relax and revitalise in the spa, with its Romanesque pool, steam room and pampering treatments, go jogging or even play boules.

Love time Splash out on a suite over the pool, complete with clawfoot bath, velvet-covered sofa and panoramic country views.

Love bites Chef Stephen Harvey's seasonal menus major on what's good and what's local. Plump for caramelised Rye Bay scallops, roasted Deal cod, Kentish partridge, Sussex venison, Romney Marsh lamb or delicious Dover sole.

Love it up You're in White Cliffs country, so make time for clifftop walks and an idle day on the beach. Leeds Castle and Canterbury are also within easy reach.

Who loves? Channel hoppers keen to round off their trip in style.

You'll love ❥ A Dover hotel with plenty to sing about.

Newick Park

Newick, East Sussex BN8 4SB
T 01825 723633
F 01825 723969
E bookings@newickpark.co.uk
W www.newickpark.co.uk
Virginia Childs

13 rooms, 3 suites
£165 to £285 per room per night
including full English breakfast
Dinner from £32.50 à la carte

Open all year

From London: head South on the A23/M23, joining the A272 to Hayward's Heath south of Cuckfield. Once at Newick, follow signs from the village green.

From the moment you turn into the sweeping drive up to Newick Park, you can't help but imagine the clattering of horse's hooves and Hanson cabs. This elegant Georgian manor is pure *Pride and Prejudice*, with everything you could want for a few days of high living: sweeping lawns, wooded grounds complete with roving peacocks and antique-filled salons. What's more, they take bedtime seriously here: expect vast king-size beds, rich drapes and finest Egyptian bedlinen, making it quite possible to lose yourself entirely under the sheets. Take a dip in the secluded outdoor pool or enjoy a spot of croquet on the lawn. Don your tweeds and go clay pigeon shooting, or in true gentry style, take a ride around the grounds. Making the most of the great outdoors here is positively encouraged, with an array of umbrellas at the ready for showery days. Whether you want to lock yourselves away in your bedroom or play out your M'Lady fantasies to the full, the friendly staff won't so much as raise an eyebrow.

Love time   Book Her Ladyship's, with its four-poster and views across the estate, or Longford, with its deep window seats made for sharing.
Love bites   Dinner is an occasion here. Try sea bass and scallops cooked on a bed of fennel, rounded off with a fresh coconut soufflé. Menus major on fresh organic produce, much of which comes from the estate itself.
Love it up   Take in regal Sheffield Park, pack a hamper and head for Glyndebourne or wind down the windows for a breezy drive on the Sussex Downs.
Who loves?   Darcys and their damsels up for country pursuits.

You'll love ❥ The grandest setting for a stately romance.

SOUTH

Amberley Castle

Amberley, nr Arundel
West Sussex BN18 9LT
T 01798 831992
F 01798 831998
E info@amberleycastle.co.uk
W www.amberleycastle.co.uk
Joy & Martin Cummings

13 rooms, 6 suites
£165 to £375 per room per night
3 course dinner from £35
A la carte dinner from £50

Open all year

From the M23 (J11): take the A264 to Horsham, then the A24 to Worthing. Turn onto the A283 for Storrington and then the B2139 for Amberley.

Amberley scooped the title of Room for Romance Hotel of the Year 2004 – and it's not hard to see why. Medieval stone walls, mullioned windows, massive oak doors and turreted towers make this 900-year-old castle in the lee of the South Downs a corker. Owners Joy and Martin Cummings have lavished attention on this atmospheric property, blending regal splendour with shameless comfort. Everything you could want in a romantic getaway is laid on here – there's even a resident ghost to send sensuous shivers down your spine. Laze in a hammock on the tiny island in a lake where koi carp bask, take each other on at croquet, or hang out in Mistletoe Lodge, the castle's new tree house. Reached by a rope bridge, this luxury thatched hideout gives a whole new meaning to "love nest"! Wait up until midnight, and you'll be treated to the spectacle of the magnificent two-tonne portcullis being lowered for the night. And so to bed...

Love time   All rooms have four-posters and whirlpool baths (naturally), but those in the know opt for the no-holds-barred Arundel and Chichester suites.

Love bites   The candlelit 12th century Queens Room is the setting for your nightly banquet. Ask for table Eight to dine like royalty on a raised dais beneath the soaring barrel-vaulted ceiling. Amberley's cuisine – with more than a dash of French finesse – pays tribute to the castle's noble heritage.

Love it up   Historic Arundel, Chichester and the Sussex beaches are close by.

Who loves?   Elizabeth I and Charles II – along with a stellar cast of modern-day celebs.

You'll love   Bedding down behind the floodlit battlements: just the place for today's knights to conquer their damsels in style.

LONDON

Go for shopping, shows and late-late clubbing
Eat a lazy champagne brunch
Take stilettos (for the bedroom, silly)
Bedtime story? a bodice-ripping yarn

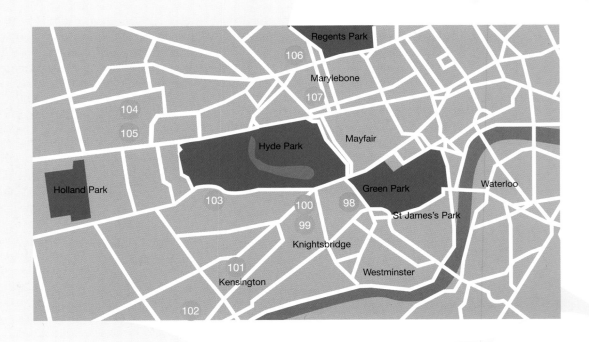

Regents Park

106

Marylebone

107

104

105

Hyde Park

Mayfair

Holland Park

103

Green Park

Waterloo

100

98

99

St James's Park

Knightsbridge

101

Westminster

Kensington

102

Pages 98-107

The Stafford

St James's Place, London SW1A 1NJ
T 020 7493 0111
F 020 7493 7121
E info@thestaffordhotel.co.uk
W www.thestaffordhotel.co.uk
Terry Holmes

67 rooms, 14 suites
£330 to £1,018 per room per night
including a bottle of house champagne
Dinner from £42.50

Open all year

The hotel is just off Piccadilly. Staff will direct you to nearby safe parking. Nearest underground station: Green Park (one stop Victoria).

Tucked away discreetly down a courtyard in regal St James's, The Stafford is a top-notch hotel that has it all: a terrific location with a wealth of West End stores and attractions on the doorstep, coupled with a rare sense of privacy and seclusion. No surprises, then, that it has picked up the accolade of No 1 London hotel from Andrew Harper's *Hideaway* report. No less than three royal residences lie within a five-minute walk, and the hotel has a distinctly clubby feel (no wonder – those in the know have been coming here for years), so guests can expect the star treatment from the moment they are greeted by the immaculately uniformed concierge. Service is discreet and unobtrusive, and jovial director Terry Holmes was recently voted the world's number one hotel manager. This is the perfect place to hide away, just minutes from the bright lights and razzamatazz of the West End.

Love time   Bed down in the 18th century mews stables, in a pretty cobbled courtyard. Perfect, as guests have noted, for a roll in the hay.

Love bites   Kick off with the perfect dry Martini in the American bar before dining on award-winning cuisine embracing modern British and classical dishes. The hotel's 350-year-old cellars house an array of rare vintages.

Love it up   London's bright lights are right on the doorstep: you're minutes from theatreland, Jermyn Street and Burlington Arcade. Those after a workout can pick up a complimentary pass for nearby Third Space health club.

Who loves?   Just look at the signed photos on the wall of the American bar!

You'll love   The perfect London hideout.

LONDON

Eleven Cadogan Gardens

11 Cadogan Gardens, Sloane Square
London SW3 2RJ
T 020 7730 7000
F 020 7730 5217
E reservations@number-eleven.co.uk
W www.11cadogan.com
Mark Fresson

54 rooms, 6 suites
£235 to £325 per room per night
Dinner from £30 per person

Open all year

The hotel is a few minutes from
Knightsbridge. Nearest underground
station: Sloane Square.

This handsome row of four Chelsea townhouses is run with all the professionalism of a top London hotel, but feels more like a top-person's private club. Indeed, it was intended for "ladies and gentlemen who can furnish suitable introductions" when it first opened many years ago. There's no reception desk, and a butler is on hand to greet you at the door. Arrive mid-afternoon and you'll find tea being served in the drawing room, where old wood panelling, antiques, fine paintings, rugs, William Morris hand-blocked wallpaper and Colefax and Fowler fabrics add to the luxurious feel. It's the very epitome of understated English good taste; a theme not forsaken in the plush bedrooms with their deliciously deep marble baths. There's a small well-equipped gym too, with a masseur on hand to administer a gentle pummelling. Staff are unfailingly charming. The hotel not only enjoys a lovely spot overlooking one of the city's most fashionable garden squares, but is strategically positioned twixt the toff's hunting grounds of Chelsea, Belgravia and Knightsbridge. We reckon Number Eleven's heaven.

Love time   The stunning Upper Garden suite looks out onto the leafy square.
Love bites   There's complimentary tea and cakes in the drawing room each afternoon, with sherry and canapés later.
Love it up   Splurge on Sloane Street or Kings Road (on the doorstep); book the best stalls seats at the Royal Court theatre (down the road); discover some Chelsea hot spots (within minutes). More London? Easily reached.
Who loves?   Those in the know – no names mentioned.

You'll love   A stylish number all round.

The Beaufort

33 Beaufort Gardens, London SW3 1PP
T 020 7584 5252
F 020 7589 2834
E reservations@thebeaufort.co.uk
W www.thebeaufort.co.uk
Ahmed Jajbhay

22 rooms, 7 suites
£155 to £325 per room per night

Open all year

The hotel is just off Brompton Road.
Nearest underground station:
Knightsbridge.

This chic pied à terre in swanky Knightsbridge overlooks a pretty tree-lined square, and can justly claim to be a perfect little hotel in a perfect place. No wonder it's been showered in awards. Art lovers will be in heaven here – the world's largest collection of English watercolour paintings adorns the walls. Although you're in the heart of the capital, The Beaufort has all the laid-back charm of a country house, and you'll be quite happy to spend hours curled up in the lounge on a sumptuous sofa, only moving to help yourself to a complimentary glass of bubbly from the residents' bar. Impeccably done out rooms are stocked with little extras like complimentary chocolates and biscuits. Feel like a breath of fresh air and a touch of culture? Staff are ready to advise on anything from theatre tickets to personal shopping, while the V&A, Science and Natural History museums are a short stroll away.

Love time   Junior suites have massive beds, comfy seating areas and posh Escada smellies in well-kitted marble bathrooms.

Love bites   Breakfast is brought to your room, so you can nibble your croissants without stirring. Complimentary afternoon tea is a no-holds-barred affair with home-made strawberry jam, fresh scones and clotted Devonshire cream. Still peckish? You're minutes from a host of superb eateries.

Love it up   Shop, shop and shop! Harvey Nicks, Harrods, Peter Jones and London's top designer boutiques are right on your doorstep.

Who loves?   Illustrious names adore this discreet Knightsbridge townhouse.

You'll love ❥ A lavish little London lovenest.

Blakes

33 Roland Gardens, South Kensington
London SW7 3PF
T 020 7370 6701
F 020 7373 0442
E blakes@blakeshotels.com
W www.blakeshotels.com
Anouska Weinberg

43 rooms, 9 suites
£275 to £950 per room per night
Dinner from £50

Open all year

The hotel is between Old Brompton Road and Fulham Road. Nearest underground station: South Kensington.

Flair and flamboyance make visually dazzling Blakes – opened and owned by Lady Anouska Weinberg – a true couture hotel. The foyer is a throwback to days of the Raj, with Edwardian trunks and rattan chairs, while deliciously decadent bedrooms are designed to seduce the senses. Choose one that's white on white on white, or others in theatrical golds and blacks. Each is an original, and ravishing colour schemes range from the vivid and dramatic to the restful and soft. Trompe l'oeil and fabric covered walls are set off by exotic silks, velvets and swagged drapery. Sensuous colour palettes are ripe with cardinal reds, lavender, vanilla and tea rose. The result melds the exquisite with the plush, where design opulence is matched by 21st century comforts. Sip a cocktail in the atmospheric bar or surface for air in the hotel's courtyard garden, before dining on beautifully presented east-west fusion cuisine in a heady and intoxicating setting. Blakes remains a sought-after and seductive lovers' hideaway – just the place to be swept away.

Love time   What's your fantasy? Bedrooms invite you to choose between the pleasures of the Orient, a 1930s cruise liner, or a sultan's harem.
Love bites   Blakes' glossy-black restaurant has been aptly described as being "like an opium den managed by Coco Chanel." Start swooning.
Love it up   You're minutes from the top Knightsbridge and Chelsea stores, and some of London's great museums.
Who loves?   Sensualists with cash to splash. "Fabulousness personified," wrote one.

You'll love   The sheer extravagance of it all.

Twenty Nevern Square

20 Nevern Square, London SW5 9PD
T 020 7565 9555
F 020 7565 9444
E hotel@twentynevernsquare.co.uk
W www.twentynevernsquare.co.uk
Faisal Saloojee

20 rooms
£100 to £195 per room per night

Open all year

Nevern Square is a short walk from Warwick Road and Cromwell Road. Nearest underground station: Earls Court.

Refinement is the keynote of this newly restored townhouse in an elegant London square. A private home converted into a smart four-star deluxe hotel, its 20 sumptuous bedrooms are decorated in a mix of Asian and European styles. A touch of class flows from the compact, fully marbled bathrooms through to the flamboyant bedrooms with their beautiful hand-crafted furniture. Take time to explore here: modern essentials, such as internet access, sit alongside old-style comforts, and the little cabinet in the corner hides a music system to complement the wide-screen TV concealed in the armoire. Nevern Square boasts a bedroom for every mood. The Chinese room has cream silk hangings at the windows and black and red silk bedspreads. The Terrace room is a private sanctuary in teal and rust tones with mahogany sleigh beds and a private terrace for breakfast à deux. And the Rococo room is a symphony to excess – as befits a hideaway so close to London's most exclusive shops.

Love time	The terraced Pasha suite is another world: wrap yourself in peacock-patterned silk as you lie back on soft velvet cushions.
Love bites	Generous breakfasts start the day here. Night owls can order the hotel's famous picnic trays for celebrating in bed or on a private terrace.
Love it up	AbFab fans will adore being just a short sprint from the shopaholic's hunting grounds of Sloane Street and Harvey Nicks. And the royal parks are almost as close.
Who loves?	Shhh... the watchword here is tact.
You'll love	Getting away from it all without leaving town.

The Baglioni

60 Hyde Park Gate, Kensington
London SW7 5BB
T 020 7368 5700
F 020 7368 5701
E info@baglionihotellondon.com
W www.baglionihotellondon.com
Luca Virgilio

16 rooms, 52 suites
£190 to £1,500 per room per night
(excluding breakfast and VAT)
Dinner from £50

Open all year

The hotel is opposite
Kensington Gardens.
Nearest underground station:
Kensington High Street.

Seductive, sultry and oozing Latin sex appeal, the Baglioni has glamour written all over it. Milanese catwalk chic has been mixed with the extravagance of a Roman palazzo right in the heart of Kensington, making it London's hottest new five-star address. Guests are greeted with a glass of chilled champagne in the stunning reception area, with its dark walls, black Venetian glass chandeliers, splashes of gold leaf and soaring silver urns. Long stemmed roses have been turned into an art form, while a montage of stills from old Fellini movies screens the circular bar. Upstairs, no-expense-spared rooms showcase the best of Italian design flair, with black lacquered wood floors, giant mirrors and surfaces glinting in burnished gold. Gorgeous bathrooms have wall-to-wall mirrors, downlit hammered steel basins and deep tubs for soaking. We loved our Illy espresso machine, not to mention the sleek LCD TVs that let you trawl through 1,500 music tracks and over 100 movies. There's a butler on call to unpack your case, hang up your clothes and press your little black number for dinner. La Dolce Vita starts here.

Love time Cancel plans to go out and splash out on a suite. You'll want to enjoy the full works.
Love bites Sleek young Italian staff notch up the glamour in the Brunello restaurant, where chef Stefano Stecca fuses market-fresh ingredients into innovative Italian cuisine – whether it's pasta, sea bass or ossobuco.
Love it up Kensington Palace and the stores of High Street Ken are outside the door.
Who loves? Hugh Grant, Penelope Cruz, Naomi Campbell and Jensen Button stay.

You'll love ▸ Sumptuous Italian style comes to Kensington.

The Portobello

22 Stanley Gardens, London W11 2NG
T 020 7727 2777
F 020 7792 9641
E info@portobello-hotel.co.uk
W www.portobello-hotel.co.uk
Tim & Cathy Herring

24 rooms
£120 to £275 per room per night
Dinner from £25

Closed Christmas and New Year

The hotel is just off Kensington Park Road. Nearest underground station: Notting Hill Gate.

Buzzy and bohemian Notting Hill – trendier than ever since the release of Roger Michell's eponymous 1999 film – is a fitting setting for London's original boutique hotel. The unique chic of the Portobello, favourite haunt of rock stars, actors and artists, perfectly sums up the raffish spirit of the area. Overlooking a pretty square, it's a neo-classical townhouse, tall and slender as a supermodel, with a narrow staircase linking the maze of 24 rooms to the colonial-style, mirrored lobby. This is a place that flaunts its eccentricities – both among the guests (Alice Cooper famously kept his pet python here) and in the exotic and magnificently comfortable bedrooms. From basement boudoirs with private courtyards to intimate attic eyries, rooms are an extravaganza of rich and moody colours, arty antiques, colourful Edwardiana, decadent clawfoot baths and diverting objets trouvés. Expect the unconventional in this hip London hideaway.

Love time   Go Moroccan, go Victorian, go Japanese, or just go to bed. We rated Room 16, with its gold and white decor and opulent *Boogie Nights*-style round bed, as the pick of the bunch.

Love bites   Nibble on tapas in the downstairs bar, or stroll through leafy Georgian terraces to sister restaurant Julie's for shamelessly romantic candlelit dining.

Love it up   You're just minutes from Portobello Road and its famous antique market, and the deliciously boutique-y shops of Westbourne Grove.

Who loves?   Kate Moss and Johnny Depp reportedly bathed here in champagne. Other stars to bed down include David Bowie, U2, Van Morrison and Tina Turner.

You'll love ❤   Boutique hotel heaven in London's trendiest neighbourhood.

LONDON

🛏 ৶ R·R

Miller's Residence

111a Westbourne Grove
London W2 4UW
T 020 7243 1024
F 020 7243 1064
E enquiries@millersuk.com
W www.millersuk.com
Martin & Ioana Miller

6 rooms, 2 suites
£150 to £230 per room per night

Open all year

The hotel is on Westbourne Grove.
Nearest underground stations: Bayswater
and Notting Hill Gate (for Paddington
and Heathrow Express).

How many curios, pictures, trinkets and objets trouvés can you cram into a square foot? If you're Martin Miller, the man behind the famous antiques bible, it's plenty. Climb the narrow stairs (walls muralled Chinoiserie-style by his wife Ioana and strewn with Old Curiosity Shop pieces), push past the sedan chair and enter the magnificently quirky first floor drawing room, glittering under dozens of candles at dusk. Everything pulls together effortlessly, and despite the profusion of objects it all feels extraordinarily restful. Complimentary drinks laid out on a George I table are available round the clock, and the owners often join their guests for a snifter. Sink languidly into one of the kilim-covered or William Morris sofas by the fire with a glass of Miller's gin and bliss out before bedtime. Individually and exquisitely styled bedrooms (one even boasts a genuine Chippendale four-poster) are named after poets. Each has a verse – be it Keats, Wordsworth or Byron – stencilled on the back of the door. Miller's is unsurprisingly a big hit with fashion photographers.That's not Kate or Naomi lurking behind some William and Mary is it?

Love time   Each antique-packed room is named after a poet. They're all dead romantic.

Love bites   Tuck into continental breakfast around a communal table. You're on the doorstep of some great ethnic eateries and trend-setting restaurants here.

Love it up   Miller's is just an amble from Portobello Road's busy antiques market, Kensington's top stores and walks in Hyde Park.

Who loves?   This place bristles with showbiz, film and fashion folk.

You'll love ▶   A one-in-a-million Aladdin's Cave.

Dorset Square

39 Dorset Square, Marylebone
London NW1 6QN
T 020 7723 7874
F 020 7724 3328
E reservations@dorsetsquare.co.uk
W www.dorsetsquare.co.uk
Wayne Davis

38 rooms
£200 to £300 per room per night
Dinner from £19.50

Open all year

The hotel is a short distance from Marylebone. Nearest underground stations: Marylebone and Baker Street (for Paddington and Heathrow Express).

Tucked away in a quiet garden square (the original 18th century Lord's Cricket Ground), this elegant Regency townhouse is marked only by an unobtrusive brass plaque. Inside, old sporting and colonial prints add a pleasingly nostalgic note, underlined by scattered books and antique furniture, and a homely sitting room perfect for settling down with the paper or a game of chess. The emphasis on low-key luxury continues from the reception area to the rooms (all brilliantly soundproofed) where flat-screen TVs, dataports and internet access blend seamlessly with traditional Sanderson drapes and button-back chairs. All have high ceilings, picture windows, huge beds and heaps of blissfully comfortable pillows. The marble bathrooms are small but well appointed with luxury toiletries and superb showers. Nice added extras include overnight shoe-cleaning, guest passes for a London health club, and an honesty bar in the morning room.

Love time   Try the Red room, whose walls, furniture and bedspread are red-hot and raring to go.

Love bites   Head down to the Potting Shed for brekkie (anything from the full British to eggs Benedict) and dinner. Menus are a trendy mix of favourites from across the world, from Thai noodles to sticky toffee pudding. A glass roof and plenty of gardening memorabilia add wit and style to the surroundings.

Love it up   Turn one way, and you can stroll through Regent's Park. Turn the other, and you're just a hop from all the stores and sights of the West End.

Who loves?   City pairs seeking tradition and a wonderfully English feel.

You'll love   Boutique charm within easy reach of London's glamour and grandeur.

LONDON

The Leonard

15 Seymour Street, London W1H 7JW
T 020 7935 2010
F 020 7935 6700
E the.leonard@dial.pipex.com
W www.theleonard.com
Tudor Hopkins

22 rooms, 21 suites
£155 to £850 per room per night

Open all year

The hotel is just off Portman Square, close to Marble Arch. Nearest underground station: Marble Arch.

It's straight out of *My Fair Lady*: four glorious 18th century townhouses with huge sash windows and wrought-iron balconies have been transformed into one of London's most discreetly luxurious hotels. The beautiful lobby is a comfortable place to relax in a sofa or armchair with a complimentary newspaper, the sitting area merging seamlessly into the café/bar, where background jazz murmurs seductively over cocktails and canapés. For those in the know, the hidden roof garden is the perfect lovers' escape and the small but beautifully formed exercise room is waiting to take your breath away. The bedrooms – a mix of rooms, suites and even fully fitted apartments – are all individually designed and decorated with exquisite fabrics and antiques, power showers in the marble bathrooms, wireless internet and DVD players. Beds are heaped high with huge pillows and even the linen has a designer pedigree. No wonder the cognoscenti rate this as a capital boutique hotel.

Love time   The sprawling (300 sq ft) first floor Grand suites hark back to an era of no-expense spared luxury. Expensive fabrics, dark woods and double height ceilings have plenty of wow.

Love bites   With the eateries of St Christopher's Place just round the corner and the West End at your feet, you won't be short of places to dine out.

Love it up   Shopping for a rock? The jewellers of Bond Street are on your doorstep.

Who loves?   This is a home-from-home for many famous sports and showbiz faces – but they don't kiss and tell!

You'll love   One of London's best kept secrets.

WEST COUNTRY & CHANNEL ISLANDS

Go for surf, sand and seashore
Eat crab sandwiches, cream teas
Take beach towels big enough for two
Bedtime story? Daphne du Maurier: *Rebecca*

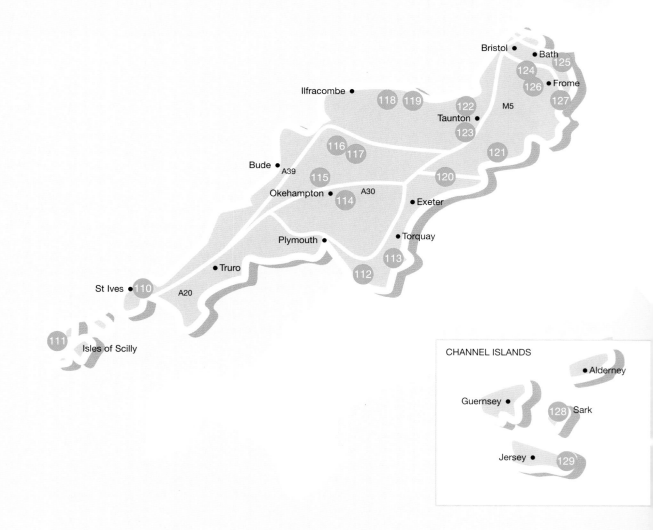

Pages 110-129

The Garrack Hotel

Burthallan Lane, St Ives
Cornwall TR26 3AA
T 01736 796199
F 01736 798955
E RR@garrack.com
W www.garrack.com
The Kilby family

18 rooms
£136 to £170 per room per night
Dinner from £21

Closed Christmas

From the A30: take the St Ives exit.
Turn onto B3311, then join the
B3306, taking the third left after a
petrol station. The hotel is
signed from here.

Cornwall's craggy coastline, breezy beaches and pretty fishing villages are its star attraction, but if you're looking for a room with a view to snuggle up in after seeing the sights, the Garrack could be the place. Set on a cliff-top overlooking the artist's colony of St Ives in the heart of Daphne du Maurier country, this is a haven of civility and old-fashioned comfort. Two acres of secluded gardens look down over the surfers' mecca of Porthmeon beach, while within the hotel's vine-clad stone walls (this 1920s residence was once known as the House on the Rock), there's plenty to do. Even on rainy days, where the crashing waves make lazy afternoons under the sheets all the more appealing, the Garrack has plenty to keep you occupied. Comfy lounges – just the place for a cream tea – are well-stocked with books and board games, while the indoor pool and spa provide an all-weather setting for a double splash-down.

Love time   Opt for Room Four's four-poster, free-standing tub and views of waves below or more contemporary Room 21's spa bath and half-tester.

Love bites   Tuck into market-fresh shellfish or the catch of the day landed at nearby Newlyn. Lobster is a speciality here and the well-priced wine list features over 70 bins.

Love it up   Explore the town's trendy galleries and bars, debate the latest exhibition at the Tate St Ives (so was it art?) and share an ice cream on the beach.

Who loves?   Actors shooting in the area and weekenders who've been coming here for years.

You'll love   Cosying up by the fire after windswept walks along the cliffs.

Hell Bay

Bryher, Isles of Scilly TR23 0PR
T 01720 422947
F 01720 423004
E contactus@hellbay.co.uk
W www.hellbay.co.uk
Euan Rodger

25 suites
£130 to £220 per person per night
Breakfast and dinner included

Closed Jan – mid Mar

Reach the Isles of Scilly by helicopter or boat from Penzance, or fly direct from various regional airports. The hotel will make all travel arrangements for you.

Hell Bay? Hell, no. Just a bit of scilliness on the part of owners Robert and Lucy Dorrien-Smith. Hell Bay clings to Bryher, a tiny foam-flecked sliver of land in the Scilly Isles overlooking an ocean that doesn't stop till it reaches America. Azure water meets wash-powder white beaches here; there are few roads but wildflowers in profusion, and above all, a peaceful immensity. Rooms are swish with Malabar fabrics and Lloyd Loom furnishings; think New England meets California with hints of the Caribbean. Reception areas boast world-class St Ives school art; Hepworth, Hitchens and Trevelyan. Suites maintain the eclectic theme and glory in vistas from private patios or balconies. Sea breezes invariably get frisky here and whip up appetites for Graham Shone's classical-meets-modern cuisine, which shines with seafood creations. Dine on steamed sea bass with Asian herbs, chargrilled tiger tail prawns or Bryher crab. You can enjoy it alfresco, sharing the views with seals, puffins and seagulls. There's a well equipped leisure area too with a gym, pool, sauna and jacuzzi. Dreamy? Yes, oh yes.

Love time　Bedrooms are made for getting fresh: think sunshine yellows, powder blues and crisp whites. Private patios and balconies offer dazzling sea views.

Love bites　Dining here is refreshingly informal. Lip-smackingly fresh cuisine casts its net wide over locally caught fish, crab and lobster – and more besides.

Love it up　Tiny island, tons to do: try watersports, boat rides, beaches and coastal paths. Island-hop to Tresco's Abbey Gardens, laze poolside or go golfing.

Who loves?　Escapists for whom heaven won't do. Oh, it's Hell.

You'll love　Soaking up England's last coastline (next stop, America).

Burgh Island

Burgh Island, Bigbury-on-Sea
South Devon TQ7 4BG
T 01548 810514
F 01548 810243
E reception@burghisland.com
W www.burghisland.com
Tony Orchard & Deborah Clark

23 rooms and suites
£275 to £420 per room per night
Dinner included

Closed 2-28 Jan

From the A38: travel towards
Plymouth, then follow signs for
Modbury and Bigbury-on-Sea.
Call the hotel from the turn-off
to arrange a pick-up.

Cut off from the mainland (forget mobile phones and unwelcome interruptions here), Burgh Island is an Art Deco haven surrounded by the seas. Think flappers in cloche hats, cads with monocles and pencil moustaches or even Baywatch with dress sense, and you are halfway there. Noël Coward adored this great escape and Agatha Christie used it as a setting for several scenes of sin and seduction in her novels. The elegant hotel and gastronomic inn have seen more than their fair share of romantic rendezvous over the years, and its setting is as flighty as a heartbeat – one moment cut off from the South Devon coast, the next linked to real life by a shimmering sandy causeway. At high tide, the sea tractor plucks guests from the mainland, bringing them to this perfectly preserved time-warp where, with Charleston lessons and wicked cocktails, the spirit of the roaring 1920s and indiscreet 30s lives on. Lovingly maintained by Tony Orchard and Deborah Clark, this really is an icon of a golden age.

Love time   Discover the potential of South Devon's biggest bed in the Garden suite.
Love bites   Classic tradition with a contemporary twist marks out dinner in the period dining room, while chef Conor Heneghan blends South Sea spices with catch of the day in The Pilchard Inn. On Valentine's Day, don black tie and pearls and dine on innuendo-laden dishes, after a rippingly good Martini.
Love it up   Learn to Charleston and tango, or climb the hill and watch for dolphins.
Who loves?   Edward came with Mrs Simpson but we can't say who stayed with Noël Coward, Gertrude Lawrence or glamorous aviatrix Amy Johnson.

You'll love   Jazzy Art Deco style on a fantasy seaside island.

Nonsuch House

Church Hill, Kingswear
Dartmouth, Devon TQ6 0BX
T 01803 752829
F 01803 752357
E enquiries@nonsuch-house.co.uk
W www.nonsuch-house.co.uk
Kit & Penny Noble

3 rooms
£90 to £110 per room per night
Dinner from £25

Open all year

From the A380 (Torquay): join the A3022, then the A379 for Dartmouth. After two miles, fork left onto the B3205. Turn left up Higher Contour Road, and continue down Ridley Hill. Nonsuch is on the seaward side at the hairpin bend.

A grand Edwardian townhouse has been converted into this terrific family-run B&B, perched on a hill with heart-stopping views across the estuary to the ancient port of Dartmouth with its castle, cottages clinging to the hillside and yachts bobbing on the tide. The stunning conservatory and terrace beckon for pre-dinner drinks, while inside, the house is cosy and intimate, with sunny colours, log fires, well-chosen fabrics and a beautifully cared-for feel. South-facing bedrooms, named after the shipping forecasts, are large and airy, bright with sunlight and reflected water all year-round. Dinner is served here four nights a week. There's a set menu, though you can always plan ahead and ask chef-patron Kit to recreate your favourite meal or a seduction special. Remember to bring your own bubbly or wine (there's no license) and the stage is set. Dartmouth is just a five-minute ferry ride away.

Love time   One room has a balcony and all have picture windows framing ever-changing sea views.

Love bites   Salmon fishcakes and home-made waffles have helped breakfasts here win awards, while peckish moments can be sated with meltingly good home-baked cakes and cookies.

Love it up   Resident labrador, Bill, will be happy to take you for walks along breezy coastal paths. The owners will rescue those he's tired out and arrange sailing, fishing and river trips.

Who loves?   Boat lovers and painters flock here, as does seafood maestro, Rick Stein.

You'll love   A chic little gem that's terrific value, too.

Blagdon Manor

Ashwater, nr. Beaworthy
Devon EX21 5DF
T 01409 211224
F 01409 211634
E stay@blagdon.com
W www.blagdon.com
Steve & Liz Morey

7 rooms
£100 per room per night
Dinner from £26

Closed two weeks Oct/Nov and Jan/Feb

From Launceston: take the A388 Holsworthy road. Pass Chapman's Well and turn right at second sign for Ashwater, then first right for Blagdon. The hotel is a few hundred yards further on.

On arrival at Steve and Liz Morey's 16th century manor, chances are two chocolate labbies, Nutmeg and Cassia, will bounce out to greet you. Wet noses deserve a pat before taking in the surrounds; fields, hedgerows and sweeping lawns merging into North Devon vistas and Dartmoor. Within, all is homely but stylish. Original features abound in this rambling Grade II Listed manor house, where heavy oak beams, old slate flagstones and a vast fireplace nudge a nice mix of period and modern pieces. Individual bedrooms benefit from prettily co-ordinated soft furnishings. Snifter before dinner? A glass decanter of sherry awaits. Steve's cooking is acknowledged and accomplished, concentrating on seasonal south-west ingredients: free-range chicken and duck, local game, Cornish seafood and West Country cheeses. He also cultivates their own kitchen garden. The Moreys – for whom nothing seems too much trouble – aim to make guests feel as if they're relaxing in the country hidey-hole of close friends. And it's well worth a stay here if your best mates fall short of these standards.

Love time   Bedrooms are both cosy and freshly colour co-ordinated, and all enjoy garden views.

Love bites   Home cooking never tasted this good: enjoy seared trout with pea mash, or brandade of salt cod and crab with roasted scallops.

Love it up   Check out the Eden Project or Falmouth's Maritime Museum, roam Dartmoor and Exmoor, follow bracing coastal paths, play golf, fish or shoot.

Who loves?   The Devonshire set. Labradors (and other canines) welcome!

You'll love   A stylish home-from-home out West.

Lewtrenchard Manor

Lewdown, nr. Okehampton
Devon EX20 4PN
T 01566 783222
F 01566 783332
E info@lewtrenchard.co.uk
W www.lewtrenchard.co.uk
Sarah Harvey

14 rooms
£140 to £250 per room per night
Dinner from £35

Open all year

From the A30: take the A386 turn-off,
turn right at bottom of slip road, then
immediately left for Lewdown.
After six miles, turn left at sign for
Lewtrenchard.

Built on foundations so old they're mentioned in the Domesday Book, this wonderful Jacobean manor is set in its own valley with 12 acres of formal gardens, woods and parkland, complete with an avenue of beech trees and swans skimming the lake. Behind its mellow West Country stone facade, Lewtrenchard's irrepressibly grand Victorian interior was designed by Reverend Sabine Baring Gould, who penned *Onward, Christian Soldiers* – one of several highly colourful characters to own the house through the ages. With its oak-panelled staircase, book-lined library, ornate plasterwork, mullioned windows and colonnaded courtyard, Lewtrenchard is as delicious as a Devon cream tea. Crisp white linen and a buzz of anticipation set the tone for modern British cuisine, superbly cooked and presented. Every bedroom is different, but all have tall windows, comfy armchairs, antique beds (some four-postered), cuddly robes and bath towels big enough for two.

Love time   Slumber in the original bed of Henrietta Maria, wife of Charles I, in Melton. Or bed down in the Bridal suite, in your own secluded tower.
Love bites   Herbs and veggies come straight from the kitchen garden, while seasonal foods from venison and guinea fowl to wild salmon are sourced locally.
Love it up   Wander through the hotel's pretty grounds or blow away the cobwebs on the wilds of Dartmoor. Do check out the Eden Project and the Lost Gardens of Heligan.
Who loves?   Mum's the word – celebrity visitors know their privacy will be protected.

You'll love ▶   Life at a Victorian country house party.

Eastacott Barton

Umberleigh, Devon EX37 9AJ
T 01769 540545
E stay@eastacott.com
W www.eastacott.com
James & Sue Murray

5 rooms, 1 cottage
£65 to £115 per room per night

Closed first two weeks Jan

From the M5 (J27): take A361 to Tiverton/Barnstaple. After 23 miles, turn left to South Molton. Fork right in village, then left to Torrington on B3227. After six miles turn left to Eastacott. Do not turn left at stone cross (marked Eastacott!) but continue for 700 yards.

Don't tell the villagers of the quiet hamlet of Eastacott, but behind those cobbled paths and neat lawns is a sanctuary of self-indulgence. Within farmhouse walls, guests luxuriate till late with a decadent weekend lie-in till 11 in a hideaway under the rafters. In fact, only the thought of what has been described as the best breakfast in England lures them from beneath sumptuous Egyptian cotton sheets to the table. Play your special song on the stereo in the bedroom and take time getting dressed. This decidedly upmarket B&B may not be a hotel, but the bathrooms are designed for serious pampering. Linger by the window to take in magnificent Taw Valley views and the heady, almost intoxicating fragrance of an English country garden. Each bedroom is named after a traditional flower – an incitement to sneak out, wander the lanes or venture on the moors to enjoy Devon at its best.

Love time   Learn how not to be too late for breakfast and still spend an extra few minutes wallowing in the Honeysuckle room's jacuzzi.

Love bites   Work up an appetite for Sue Murray's traditional breakfast: home-made fruit compote, fresh-baked loaves and croissants, smoked haddock and more. Stay in the farmhouse's self-catering cottage and you can knock up your own dinner à deux.

Love it up   Take the Tarka country rail line, or shop for champagne flutes at nearby Dartington Crystal.

Who loves?   Lovers who want to escape the limelight and squirrel under the sheets.

You'll love   The timelessness of a rural England the world has seemingly passed by.

Northcote Manor

Burrington, nr. Umberleigh
Devon EX37 9LZ
T 01769 560501
F 01769 560770
E rest@northcotemanor.co.uk
W www.northcotemanor.co.uk
Cheryl Hinksman

11 rooms
£140 to £240 per room per night
Dinner from £35

Open all year

From Exeter: take the A377 towards Barnstaple. The entrance to the estate is directly off the road, opposite the Portsmouth Arms.

RR

Here we are in rural North Devon following a long driveway that meanders through 20 acres of woods, gardens and lawns to wisteria-clad and centuries-old Northcote Manor – a handsome, mellow-stoned Georgian pile in an idyllic woodland setting. Expectations of country-house peace and deep comforts are about to be realised – and how. A zesty yellow hallway leads guests inside to polished wood floors with rugs, drop-in sofas, books, flowers and a crackling fire. A striking backdrop of hand-painted murals in the drawing room and dining room highlight the Manor's associations with Tavistock Abbey a thousand years ago. After leisurely pre-dinner drinks we sailed into the smart pinky-glow restaurant nicely set up for chef Richie Herke's prize-winning cuisine. His versatility also includes excellent wedding banquets (the hotel can be hired exclusively for nuptials), while the Dine & Stay option allows diners to enjoy and imbibe with unhurried relish, then slip upstairs with a half-bottle of champers for breakfast. Staff are adept at putting guests at ease, and promise cares will slip away. Believe us, they do.

Love time   The Manor suite has a jacuzzi and an oriental vibe, while Orchard enjoys valley views and a window table for just-out-of-bed breakfasts.

Love bites   Go gourmet here, with winners such as seared king scallops, Cornish turbot fillet, and caramelised apricots with panna cotta. Sheer indulgence.

Love it up   Unwind with in-house aromatherapy and beauty treatments, or head outdoors for golf, tennis, fishing, racing and croquet.

Who loves?   *Just a Minute* host Nicholas Parsons.

You'll love   The cream of North Devon.

The Rising Sun

Harbourside, Lynmouth
Devon EX35 6EG
T 01598 753223
F 01598 753480
E reception@risingsunlynmouth.co.uk
W www.risingsunlynmouth.co.uk
Tony & Clair Vickery

16 rooms,
£98 to £138 per room per night
Dinner from £30

Open all year

From the M5 (J23): take the A39
to Lynmouth. The Rising Sun is
next to the harbour.

Step inside this thatched 14th-century inn, and its uneven oak floors, thick limed walls, wood panelling and crooked ceilings take you back through centuries of buccaneering, smuggling and tales from the sea. Verdant hills bordered by flowered gardens rise up behind the hotel, while at the front it peers over a small stone harbour and salmon river. Owners Tony and Clair Vickery have lovingly preserved the patina of antiquity here but pepped it up with all of today's comforts. Many rooms have half-tester beds swathed in thick designer chintz, while outside you can inhale the heady scent of clambering myrtle. Dinner is served in the candlelit oak-panelled dining room whose leaded windows frame views of the highest cliffs in England. You might just catch sight of a stag or see a flash of emerald green as a kingfisher takes to the wing in scenic Lynmouth Bay. This is Devon at its chocolate-box loveliest.

Love time Plump for supposedly haunted Shelley's Cottage in the grounds, where unsuspecting souls have been awoken by a fond smack on the bottom – or so they say.

Love bites Dine on mouthwatering local Lynmouth Bay lobster, landed at the door, Exmoor venison, and salmon fished from the River Lyn. De-lish.

Love it up Stride out across the windy hills of Exmoor, visit the dramatic Doone Valley or simply hang out and watch life around the pretty little harbour.

Who loves? RD Blackmore wrote several chapters of *Lorna Doone* here, while the poet Shelley – enraptured by the setting – honeymooned here in 1812.

You'll love Melodrama and romance in a Devon lovenest.

The Oaks

Porlock, West Somerset TA24 8ES
T 01643 862265
F 01643 863131
E info@oakshotel.co.uk
W www.oakshotel.co.uk
Tim & Anne Riley

8 rooms
£120 per room per night
Four course dinner £30

Closed Dec – end Feb
(open Christmas/New Year)

From Lynmouth: travel via the A39. The hotel lies six miles east of Lynmouth and a quarter of a mile from the village.

This gabled Edwardian country house, set among lawns and ancient trees, generates an air of rural contentment. Owners Tim and Anne Riley combine all the professionalism of a hotel with the carefree comforts of home, and guests love to cosy up in the hallway's fireside snug or the pretty sitting room and bar. Period furniture, muted colours and pleasing print fabrics create a William Morris feel in salons and bedrooms that's very much in keeping with the age of the house. Guest rooms have welcoming extra touches such as fruit, flowers and magazines. The Oaks looks out across the thatched village of Porlock to the rolling hills of Exmoor and the glistening waters of Porlock Bay. Everything from the breakfast marmalade to the after-dinner chocs are made on the spot, and guests enjoy what's been described as "uncomplicated dinner party cooking at its best." Crisp with damask and crystal, the dining room offers stunning sunset views on summer evenings. Keep watching as dusk falls and you may even see a stag or playful badgers.

Love time   Comfy beds, antique furniture, picture windows, sea views and bedside tipples may make you want to bunker down for the duration.

Love bites   Daily-changing four-course menus offer choices that might feature Cornish scallops, Devon beef with avocado salsa and organic Exmoor lamb. The world's vineyards are well represented too.

Love it up   Take a camera, paints or walking shoes. From the wild Exmoor coast to seabird lagoons and National Trust gardens, the landscape is extraordinary.

Who loves?   Second honeymooners love it here. So will you.

You'll love   A terrific cosseting – and a sense that nothing is too much trouble.

Combe House Hotel & Restaurant

Gittisham, Honiton, nr. Exeter
Devon EX14 3AD
T 01404 540400
F 01404 46004
E stay@thishotel.com
W www.thishotel.com
Ruth & Ken Hunt

15 rooms
£148 to £320 per room per night
Dinner from £38

Open all year

From the M5 (J28/29): take the A373/A30 to Honiton (A303/A30 from London), then the A375 to Sidmouth and Gittisham. The hotel is happy to collect guests at Honiton Station or Exeter Airport.

A magnificent Elizabethan manor hidden deep within acres of lyrical Devon countryside, it's easy to see why Combe House – our runner-up Hotel of the Year 2003 – oozes romance. From the ancient cedar trees to the oak panelled walls, ancestral portraits, flamboyant flowers, squashy sofas and roaring log fire in the Great Hall, this serene, antique-filled house exudes a warmth and welcome. Watch the Arab horses and pheasants roam freely, explore the scented corners of hidden gardens, and drink in timeless Devon views. Every room is individually decorated with small, quirky touches; beds are dressed with softest linens and hand-made patchwork quilts. Search out hidden coves on secret beaches along the World Heritage coastline nearby, and be sure to make time for some chilled champagne while watching the sun go down.

Love time   Cuddle under the canopy of a four-poster bed in the Willington suite or unwind in the new Garden suite, with its lush sunken bath and private walled garden.

Love bites   Master chef Philip Leach uses seasonal vegetables and aromatic herbs home-grown in the gardens at Combe. Tuck into pan-roasted partridge or stun the senses with a sensual trio of chocolate, and a glass of vintage Chablis.

Love it up   Stride out over the rugged open spaces of Dartmoor or stroll down the winding drive to the chocolate-box cob and thatch village of Gittisham.

Who loves?   Lovebirds keen to slow down, switch off and recharge.

You'll love ▸ Bedding down in a sumptuous Devon hideaway.

WEST COUNTRY

The Old Rectory

Cricket Malherbie, nr. Ilminster
Somerset TA19 0PW
T 01460 54364
F 01460 57374
E info@malherbie.co.uk
W www.malherbie.co.uk
Patricia & Michael Fry-Foley

5 rooms
£85 to £95 per room per night
Dinner from £30

Closed Christmas

From the A303: take the A358 towards Chard at Horton Cross roundabout. Turn left (signed Ilminster) after two miles, then right into a lane (signed Cricket Malherbie) after a mile. The Old Rectory is a mile further.

Even finding this 16th century thatched stone rectory is fun as you follow leafy lanes to the conservation hamlet of Cricket Malherbie, nudging an Area of Outstanding Natural Beauty. And inside the flagged hallway it's just how you'd expect a storybook village rectory to look – all carved Tudor beams, uneven floors, oak furniture and book-laden shelves. This is very much a family home, and hosts Michael and Patricia Fry-Foley run the place on house party lines. Guests are made to feel more like old friends than visitors, and there's plenty of banter after dark, making it well worth staying in for the evening. Linen tablecloths, fine bone china and silver cutlery give dinner a real sense of occasion, while pretty garden views underline the rustic air. Each of the five bedrooms is decorated in its own style; guests slumber in rural peace and awaken to the birds. Should we say more? That wouldn't be cricket.

Love time Room One is a favourite, with its canopied bed and Gothic windows framing views of the country garden below.

Love bites Dining is dinner party style, with guests seated together around the large dining table. A set menu (complemented by an imaginative wine list) majors on local specialities such as West Country lamb, smoked eel, cheeses and Somerset apples.

Love it up Tour the gardens of Montacute House and East Lambrook Manor or watch the crashing waves from the Cob at Lyme Regis.

Who loves? Sociable duos who still can't resist slipping off upstairs.

You'll love Pretty house, pretty garden – pretty magic.

The Mount Somerset

Lower Henlade, Taunton
Somerset TA3 5NB
T 01823 442500
F 01823 442900
E info@mountsomersethotel.co.uk
W www.mountsomersethotel.co.uk
Barbara Loadwick

7 rooms, 4 suites
£135 to £225 per room per night
Dinner from £27.50

Open all year

From the M5 (J25): take the A358.
The hotel is two miles
along the road.

Oh the finery of a classic English country house! Built in 1805, the Mount Somerset has all the Regency curves, soaring ceilings and sweeping staircases you could yearn for – with the pleasing informality of a sociable country home. Blazing log fires, plump cushions, sumptuous fabrics and ornate plasterwork are set off by a baby grand piano for impromptu serenading, with live recitals at the weekends. But it's upstairs that this hotel really comes into its own. Sink into the deepest mattresses in elegant four-postered rooms with views over rolling Somerset hills, where marble bathrooms come with whirlpool baths and grand drapery adds to the sense of splendour. There's croquet on the lawn where the resident peacock struts his stuff, and even a helipad for making a grand arrival. Many of the hotel's guests come to the Mount to simply chill, and you can easily while away a lazy afternoon curled up on one of the comfy sofas lapping up views of the surrounding Quantock hills.

Love time   Book the four-poster Barrington suite for double bubbles in the outsize whirlpool bath.

Love bites   Candlelit dining is a must here, with local produce featuring highly on a classic yet imaginative menu.

Love it up   Sweep each other off your feet – literally – with a pleasure flight from the hotel's helipad to check out Cheddar Gorge, cliffy Charmouth and wildest Exmoor from the skies.

Who loves?   Country lovers after sumptuous Somerset style.

You'll love ▶ A place to switch off and live the moment.

RR

Bindon Country House

Langford Budville, Wellington
Somerset TA21 0RU
T 01823 400070
F 01823 400071
E stay@bindon.com
W www.bindon.com
Lynn & Mark Jaffa

12 rooms
£115 to £215 per room per night
Dinner from £35

Open all year

From the M5 (J26): take the A38 and B3187 to Wellington. Follow signs to Langford Budville, then turn right at the sharp "S" bend and follow signs to the hotel.

This 17th century mansion, tucked away behind Langford Heath's woodland nature reserve filled with generations of wild flowers, has only recently been rescued from its Sleeping Beauty slumbers by owners Mark and Lynn Jaffa. Lovingly restored, this is a grand place, with deep sofas, fireside armchairs and a grand piano to set the mood for a memorable stay. Bindon, a stone's throw from rugged moors and coastal cliffs, dates back to the Domesday book. Home through the ages to distinguished local families and military heroes, it's a stylish country house, with its wood-panelled walls, elegant wall hangings, galleried staircase and swish open-air pool. Echoes of the era of Jane Austen, croquet lawns and weekend house parties linger here. Don't be fooled by the bedrooms being named after famous battles. With a Victorian bath designed for two and a canopied four-poster bed in the Busaco room, the mood in this flamboyantly styled country house is definitely made for loving, not fighting.

Love time Comfortable, spacious rooms underline the house motto: "je trouve bien."

Love bites Tables in the alluring Wellesley restaurant gleam with polished silver and flickering candles. Chef Mike Davies' daily-changing tasting menus are focused around the seasons, with an emphasis on local ingredients. Be sure to leave room for divine lemon curd ice cream and chocolatey puds.

Love it up Explore nearby Dunster Castle, wander through Hestercombe Gardens or go hot-air ballooning above Exmoor.

Who loves? A gentleman never tells.

You'll love ❥ The intimate feel of a wood-panelled hunting lodge, in deepest Somerset.

Ston Easton Park

Ston Easton, nr. Bath
Somerset BA3 4DF
T 01761 241631
F 01761 241377
E info@stoneaston.co.uk
W www.stoneaston.co.uk
Andrew Chantrell

22 rooms
£175 to £395 per room per night
Dinner from £39.50

Open all year

From the M4 (J18): take the A46
towards Bath then the A39 towards
Shepton Mallet to join the
A37 southbound.
The hotel is signed off this road.

And so to bed: under swoops and swathes of fine fabrics draping a coronet or classic four-poster, with moonlight glancing off glass chandeliers and a seductive scent of wild flowers at the bedside. Ston Easton Park makes bedtime a treat, whether it's upstairs or down. In the Palladian grandeur and majesty of the great house, goodnight is said amid gilded sconces, moulded ceilings and trappings of aristocracy, pampering is standard and the sweeping lawn gives guests the feeling of owning one of the great country house hotels of Europe. Buried in the grounds is a 17th century gardener's cottage on the banks of the River Norr. Look out of the bedroom window after dark to see badgers and foxes rustling through the woods. Should you decide to leave the spacious bedrooms in house or cottage, indulge in gracious living in the palatial salons, dine in the Regency styled Yellow room or the award-winning Cedar Tree dining room, and invite the waiter to raid the wine cellars for a very special vintage treat.

Love time Sleep in an original Chippendale four-poster in the Master bedroom, then wallow in a bathtub fragranced by herbs and flowers from the grounds.

Love bites The original Georgian kitchen, with its polished copper pans, hints at the quality of Michael Parke's classic English fare with a continental twist to wilt willpower at 40 paces. The wine list, too, is a testament to temptation.

Love it up Sweep your lover off in one of the hotel's fleet of classic cars: take to the open roads in an Aston Martin, Ferrari or Bentley.

Who loves? The great and the good have sported here since the 18th century.

You'll love Spaniels Sorrel and Sweep – who are shameless at asking for walkies.

The Windsor Hotel

69 Great Pulteney Street, Bath BA2 4DL
T 01225 422100
F 01225 422550
E sales@bathwindsorhotel.com
W www.bathwindsorhotel.com
Cary & Sachiko Bush

14 rooms
£85 to £195 per room per night
Dinner from £25

Closed Christmas

From the M4 (J18): take the A46 into
Bath via London Road.
The hotel is reached via Bathwick Street.

Bath needs no introduction as Britain's best-preserved Georgian city (and don't forget the Romans got here first – relics of both eras have made it a World Heritage site). And the Windsor, a splendidly converted Grade I Regency townhouse in one of Europe's most elegant boulevards, makes a brilliant base right at the heart of things. If the sedan chair outside doesn't whisk you back 200 years, you could easily imagine Jane Austen society gossiping in the drawing room. The hotel's 14 ensuite bedrooms – all fresh as a new pin – are done out in trad country house style, with boldly patterned chintz and immaculate bathrooms. What come as a surprise though is the Japanese restaurant downstairs. Sakura overlooks its own garden of white pebbles and bamboo, and very serene it is too. Three styles of classical cuisine exemplify all that's delicate and delicious about the country's cuisine. Try the fondue pot, which lends itself to some saucy sharing. Then decide if Jane Austen's Bath really was the epitome of restrained passion.

Love time   Bed down in a richly draped four-poster looking out on Georgian facades.
Love bites   Go Japanese here and canoodle over udon noodles, sukiyaki and sake.
Love it up   Bathe in Bath's glories; the restored Roman baths await discovery, together with strolls around quiet crescents and Georgian squares. There are fabulous museums, cafes and antique shops, not to mention easy access to the shires and spires.
Who loves?   Literary types and thespians adore this place.

You'll love   This Regency townhouse on Bath's best-known boulevard is just dandy.

Charlton House & Monty's Spa

Charlton Road, Shepton Mallet
Somerset BA4 4PR
T 01749 342008
F 01749 346362
E enquiry@charltonhouse.com
W www.charltonhouse.com
Michael Conrad-Pickles

25 rooms
£165 to £425 per room per night
Dinner from £49.50

Open all year

From Shepton Mallet: take the A361
towards Frome. The hotel is
a mile down the road, on the left-hand
side just off the A361.

Charlton House has style in spades – and fans of the Mulberry luggage label will love the luxury and look of this mellow West Country manor house. Rich colours, wood panelling, rugs and polished floors are mixed with flair and panache, and the place exudes a sense of lavish country-house comfort. Step inside the rich burgundy and rolled-gold hall, with its family photographs and racing memorabilia, and you'll feel as if you have arrived at an Edwardian house party. Bedrooms, where soft, lived-in colours blend seamlessly with antiques, original art and quirky curios (the Roberts radio is a nice touch), are designed for slumber and seclusion. Chef Adam Fellows' impressive repertoire of dishes in the Michelin-starred Mulberry restaurant, with its ochre walls and kaftan-hooded chairs, is sure to dazzle. As if all that's not enough, a visit to Monty's, the hotel's stunning new spa, is the place to bliss out in a sculpted indoor/outdoor hydrotherapy pool, a crystal-infused steam room and scented experience showers. Spend a day here, and you'll be feeling like the cat that got the cream.

Love time Splash out on the Adam and Eve room, with its 16th century carved four-poster and opulent burgundy velvet throw. Eden indeed.

Love bites Look forward to innovative and stylish cooking with brilliant original takes on traditional dishes. There's an exceptional wine list, too.

Love it up Book a Couple's Retreat at Monty's, complete with champers and side-by-side treatments. Your credit cards may tremble, but this is OTT bliss.

Who loves? Shameless hedonists after the full Monty.

You'll love The quintessential English country house experience.

Babington House

Babington, nr. Frome
Somerset BA11 3RW
T 01373 812266
F 01373 812112
E enquiries@babingtonhouse.co.uk
W www.babingtonhouse.co.uk
Nick Jones

28 rooms
£215 to £395 per room per night
Dinner from £20

Open all year

From the M3 (J8): head for Warminster
via A303, A360 and A36. Continue
via A362 to Longleat and Frome.
The hotel will supply detailed directions
(via Mells, Coleford and Kilmersdon)
from here.

Soho meets Somerset at Babington House, the hotel that blazed a trail for a new generation of rustic chic. Hip and media-savvy, it's a stylish rework of the trad country house theme on 21st century lines – and the perfect place for anyone suffering from chintz overload. With its chilled atmosphere, laid-back clientele and nothing's-too-much-trouble young staff, Babington is as unstuffy as it gets. Dress codes don't exist, and rooms are designed with naughty weekends in mind: expect extravagant double beds piled with pillows, decadent bathrooms, a Dualit toaster and all the techno stuff – plasma screen TVs with every channel, DVDs and internet access. The Cowshed spa is the place for some serious lazing, and even has a pool that lets you swim out in the elements amid drifts of steam in basking temperature water. Treatments are taken in log cabins dotted around the lakeside, and our side-by-side massage in the Mongolian yurt left us totally blissed out. Babington House clones may be springing up fast around the country, but this is the original – and a class act.

Love time Bathrooms are made for playtime, with party showers, huge sunken or free-standing baths and oodles of bubbles, gels and pampering lotions.

Love bites Whether it's grilled Exmoor lamb, Iranian caviar or a wood-oven baked pizza, cooking is top-notch. Chink glasses in the adults-only Martini bar.

Love it up With a cinema, gym, yoga deck, bikes, tennis courts and hammocks dotting the lawns, you won't want to leave the place.

Who loves? Media types. Zoe Ball and Norman Cook were famously wed here.

You'll love ▶ That bedside pot of Raging Bull massage oil. Say no more.

La Sablonnerie

Little Sark, via Guernsey
Channel Islands GY9 0SD
T 01481 832061
F 01481 832408
W www.sablonnerie.com
Elizabeth Perrée

20 rooms, 2 suites
£119 to £175 per room per night
Dinner from £25

Closed late Oct – late April

From Guernsey: ferries operate to Sark. Guests can be collected from the harbour and taken to the hotel by a vintage horse-drawn barouche.

Draw up at the front door in a horse-drawn barouche on this pint-sized island where cars are forbidden, the land is ablaze with flowers in spring and the sea gleams turquoise and lapis. Elizabeth Perrée's ancestors have been here since 1565 and she and her family (her father, Philip, mans the granite-walled bar) are eager to show you true island hospitality. The hotel, a low-rise 16th-century farm with roses rambling across the whitewashed walls, has been carefully and cosily modernised, blending sophistication of comfort with simplicity of style. Low beams hang sturdily above beds dressed in crisp cotton sheets and wool blankets, with fresh flowers and good soaps adding to the feel-good vibe. Above all, it's the friendliness that captivates guests here snug around the crackling fire.

Love time Make hay in Room 14, a delightful converted stable with a high beamed ceiling, polished oak floors and an enticingly big bed.

Love bites With butter, beef and produce from the hotel's own farm, freshly caught Sark lobster and decadent cream teas, the food – great for the tastebuds and bad for the waistline – is far too good to pass up.

Love it up Only a mile wide and three and a half miles long, it doesn't take long to explore Sark. Let Elizabeth suggest hidden swimming bays, dramatic clifftop views and lush gardens. Hire a bicycle or horse for the ride.

Who loves? Sark poet Algernon Swinburne. "Small, sweet world of wave-encompassed wonder," he mused.

You'll love Some 400 years of history in the palm of your hand.

CHANNEL ISLANDS

Longueville Manor

St Saviour, Jersey
Channel Islands JE2 7WF
T 01534 725501
F 01534 731613
E info@longuevillemanor.com
W www.longuevillemanor.com
Malcolm Lewis

27 rooms, 3 suites
£180 to £800 per room per night
Dinner from £45

Open all year

From Jersey Airport: take the A1 to St Helier and pass through tunnel. Join the A3 towards Gorey and the hotel is just over a mile further. Over 50 flights a day from 25 UK airports serve Jersey.

Jersey's swishest hotel sits pretty in lush green countryside a few miles from the cliffs and coastal paths of this inviting island and just a short hop from the Normandy coast. Guarding its own private wooded valley, the handsome stone-built manor house – parts of which date back to the 13th century – is a luxurious haven of civility, with the added enticement of first-rate award-winning cuisine. The graciously restored interior glows with carved oak panelling, rich fabrics, warm colours and fine antiques. Sprawling bedrooms combine elegant good taste with every modern comfort, while well-drilled staff provide impeccable service. Outside, a heated pool invites guests to make the most of Jersey's sunny climate, with poolside summer dining. Guests who would sooner keep their toes dry can feed the Mandarin ducks and black swans in the lake in the pretty grounds. Splendid dinners are served in the Oak room, where home-grown produce and herbs grace menus combining the best of British and French cuisine. The Manor's master sommelier will guide you through the extensive wine list.

Love time   Shut the door to your very own turret: the Honeymoon suite awaits.
Love bites   Chef Andrew Baird's inspired cooking makes the most of Jersey's rich waters, with oysters and fresh fish star-studding an exceptional menu.
Love it up   Check out the exotic animal life at the Durrell Wildlife zoo – a mini Madagascar where endangered species thrive. Then there's Elizabeth Castle – reached by a causeway – and all that tax-free shopping.
Who loves?   Well-heeled weekenders.

You'll love ❥ The jewel in Jersey's hotel crown.

WALES

Go for green valleys, great rugby, grand language
Eat lamb, leeks and Welsh cakes
Take naughty lingerie (go off the rails in Wales)
Bedtime story? Dylan Thomas: *Under Milk Wood*

Pages 132-141

The Bell at Skenfrith

Skenfrith, Monmouthshire NP7 8UH
T 01600 750235
F 01600 750525
E enquiries@skenfrith.co.uk
W www.skenfrith.co.uk
William & Janet Hutchings

8 rooms
£95 to £170 per room per night
Dinner from £28

Closed two weeks in Jan/Feb

From the M4 (J24): take the A449/A40 to Monmouth and A466 towards Hereford. After four miles, turn left onto the B4521 towards Abergavenny. The Bell is a further three miles.

If music be the food of love, play mellow jazz and blues in the background. And if the food is just as important as the Miles Davis soundtrack, make sure you've booked a stay at this Welsh Inn of the Year, where even breakfast is a gastronomic occasion. Mind you, the food has to be great to tempt guests out of the whimsically-named bedrooms. Mood lighting, CD and DVD players and scrumptious chocolate shortbread set the tone here, while window seats and pamper-grade bathrooms take some beating. However, with oak beams, antique furniture and sumptuous sofas, the bar is a lure in itself. As to the restaurant, this is the foodies' choice where some of the world's most famous chefs come to indulge on a night off. Seasonal dishes, washed down with shrewdly selected wines and some fabulous local ales, mark the Bell at Skenfrith as a place where lingering at the table is regarded as an art.

Love time   For that romantic tryst, choose an attic suite with its own sitting room.
Love bites   From the cappuccino of wild mushrooms with tarragon and white truffle oil to the Monmouthshire lamb in redcurrant jus and white chocolate and vanilla creme brulée, lunch and dinner are occasions in waiting. But breakfast is not to be outdone: eggs Florentine or pancakes with maple syrup and smoked bacon are worth getting out of bed for.
Love it up   Meet the locals at the bar of this inviting coaching inn or feel the breeze in your face as you explore the castles of the Welsh Marches.
Who loves?   Celebrity chefs Gordon Ramsay and Raymond Blanc come for the food.

You'll love ▸ Consigning the diet to history.

Egerton Grey Country House

Porthkerry, Barry
South Glamorgan CF62 3BZ
T 01446 711666
F 01446 711690
E info@egertongrey.co.uk
W www.egertongrey.co.uk
Richard Morgan-Price

10 rooms
£110 to £140 per room per night
Dinner from £19

Open all year

From the M4 (J33): follow signs to
Cardiff-Wales Airport, then Porthkerry.
After 500 yards turn left at the hotel sign.

Through a misty valley, past an elegant Victorian viaduct, and beyond to the rugged Welsh coast – that's the kind of hand-in-hand stroll you'll be able to take from Egerton Grey, which has been described as the ultimate country house hotel. Your hosts Richard and Huw certainly believe in attention to detail. Just a short drive from Cardiff Airport, this one-time Victorian rectory is replete with old oak panelling, lovingly selected furniture, polished brass, open fireplaces, art and ornaments. Impeccable taste shines from every room – and of course Richard and Huw's vintage Rolls Royce adds to the feeling of sheer extravagance. The seven acres of lush gardens, too, bloom with old-fashioned elegance, from the croquet lawn to the giant copper beech and pastel-hued flowerbeds. Your time here is marked by the gentle ticking and musical chimes of a collection of antique clocks – and it's sure to fly by, even though the owners order you to do as little as possible!

Love time   One of the two master bedrooms has a magnificent Victorian four-poster.

Love bites   You'll dine in the former billiard room on classic home-grown or locally sourced ingredients prepared with care. Breakfast is extra special here – well worth getting dressed for.

Love it up   If you've had enough of country-house languor, the attractions of happening Cardiff Bay are just a 30-minute drive away.

Who loves?   This is a favourite among couples looking for an intimate wedding venue, or a stylish first night.

You'll love ▸   Champagne cocktails in the Edwardian drawing room – this is the life!

Penally Abbey

Penally, nr. Tenby
Pembrokeshire SA70 7PY
T 01834 843033
F 01834 844714
E info@penally-abbey.com
W www.penally-abbey.com
Steve & Elleen Warren

12 rooms
£130 to £160 per room per night
Dinner from £34

Closed Christmas

From the M4 (J49): follow
signs for A40, A477, then Tenby.
Turn off the A4139 Tenby-Pembroke
coast road into Penally.
The hotel is on the village green.

The monks always knew how to pick a good location, building their sixth century abbey high above Carmarthen Bay with views to stir the pulse. Nothing remains to mark their passing and Penally Abbey is a mainly 17th century building with a monastic tranquillity and an air of conviviality inherited from the Jameson whiskey family (also former owners). These days, Steve and Elleen Warren work hard to imbue the large, airy and elegant antique-filled rooms with a sense of laid-back comfort. The five acres of gardens and woods are perfect for a relaxed ramble past the ruined 18th century chapel. Indoors, you could take a leisurely swim in the small heated pool or tickle the ivories at the grand piano. Rooms in the main house have superb sea views, but those in the coach house are equally welcoming, with touches such as complimentary sherry and thick towelling robes. Many have four-poster beds.

Love time   Inviting rooms have lavishly draped four-poster and canopied beds, with nicely appointed bathrooms.

Love bites   The monks would have heartily approved of the Welsh regional cooking and well-stocked cellars here – though the glittering crystal, candlelight and flowers in the pretty dining room may have been a tad too much.

Love it up   Tenby's golden sands are a stone's throw away, while the 180-mile Pembrokeshire coastal path meanders nearby. Caldey Island, Laugharne (home to Dylan Thomas), Tenby and four castles are within easy reach.

Who loves?   London luvvies: among them Timothy Spall and Anthea Turner.

You'll love ♥   Living the good life on the Pembroke coast.

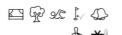

Wolfscastle Country Hotel

Wolfscastle, nr. Haverfordwest
Pembrokeshire SA62 5LZ
T 01437 741225
F 01437 741383
E enquiries@wolfscastle.com
W www.wolfscastle.com
Andrew Stirling

24 rooms
£79 to £107 per room per night
Dinner from £17.50

Closed Christmas

From the M4 (J49): take the A48/A40 to Haverfordwest, then turn right before town for Fishguard and travel a further six miles to Wolfscastle village.

Still known locally by its original name "Allt yr Afon" (don't worry, those Welsh words will be rolling off your tongue in no time), this creeper-clad country house is perfect for lovers looking for unpretentious comfort in breezy coastal surroundings. Whether you fancy exploring Pembrokeshire's 200 stunning miles of clifftop paths, picnicking on secluded beaches, spotting dolphins and puffins along the coast or snuggling up in your four-poster with the Do Not Disturb sign on the door, the friendly staff will help ensure that your stay is a treat. In fact, owner-manager Andrew Stirling and his team have been cosseting guests here for over 20 years. The restaurant here is a class act and well worth getting dressed up for, so do bring a hearty appetite to dinner. Those in the know have been keeping this rustic hotel their secret for years. Sorry, folks – we just had to let it out.

Love time   The new Executive rooms are as stylish as they come.
Love bites   What a menu! Elegant dishes prepared with top-quality local ingredients rub shoulders here with traditional pub grub. So depending on your mood, go for pan-fried fillet of halibut wrapped in parma ham, served on a bed of sautéed potatoes, spinach and crispy capers with balsamic dressing, or simply hearty cod and chips.
Love it up   Forget the Bahamas – with a bit of exploring you'll find a secluded cove perfect for that desert island fantasy.
Who loves?   Stylish couples looking for luxury that won't break the bank.

You'll love   A Welsh hideaway miles from the rat race, with cosmopolitan cuisine.

The Lake Country House

Llangammarch Wells
Powys LD4 4BS
T 01591 620202
F 01591 620457
E info@lakecountryhouse.co.uk
W www.lakecountryhouse.co.uk
Jean-Pierre & Jan Mifsud

19 rooms
£150 to £245 per room per night
Dinner from £37.50

Open all year

From the M4 (J24): take the A449/A40 for Abergavenny and Brecon, then the A470 for Builth Wells. Join the A483 West (marked LLandovery). The hotel is signed from Garth.

Tranquillity and charm are twin hallmarks of this elegant and airy neo-Tudor country house, built in 1900 as a hunting and fishing lodge in a blissfully secluded corner of mid Wales. Inside, gleaming floorboards and terracotta walls are perfect foils for the oriental rugs, dark wood antiques, expansive sofas, jugs of fresh flowers and old ticking clocks. Bedrooms are supremely comfortable, while a maitre d' in tails oversees the graciously appointed dining room. Outside, it's a visual feast and the perfect place for dreamy riverside walks or a game of croquet. Step onto dazzling precision-mown lawns that sweep down to the River Irfon – just one feature of the gorgeous grounds with 50 acres of woodlands and a well-stocked trout lake where herons and kingfishers swoop. The Lake's traditional afternoon teas – served on a trolley under the chestnut trees in summer or before a crackling fire in winter – are worth driving miles for.

Love time   You'll have your own jacuzzi bath in the beautifully furnished Eugenie suite. Soak awhile before sinking into your richly carved mahogany bed.

Love bites   An award-winning fusion of Welsh and English cuisine with an added pinch of inspiration makes dinner a winner. Try specialities such as stuffed saddle of rabbit with puy lentils, garlic confit and a light sherry vinegar jus.

Love it up   Local attractions include Powys Castle, the book emporia of Hay-on-Wye and the Brecon Beacons. There's tennis, fishing and golfing in the grounds.

Who loves?   Kaiser Wilhelm and his empress stayed here incognito in the early days. Today's celebrities also guard their anonymity carefully.

You'll love   Birdsong and seclusion in a swoon-worthy setting.

WALES

Lake Vyrnwy

Llanwddyn, nr. Welshpool
Powys SY10 0LY
T 01691 870692
F 01691 870259
E res@lakevyrnwy.com
W www.lakevyrnwy.com
Anthony Rosser

35 rooms
£155 to £220 per room per night
Dinner included

Closed one week in Feb

From Welshpool: take the A490 to
Llanfyllin, then the B4393. The hotel is
signed from Llanwddyn.

The name may look tongue-twisting (say Vern-wy) but the setting's magical. You'd be hard pushed to find dreamier surrounds than the sprawling 24,000 acre estate ringing this supremely sited country house hotel in the depths (or rather the heights) of Wales's Berwyn Mountains. Lake Vyrnwy's views alone are enough reason to stay. Wooded hills and mountain moorlands tumble down into the brilliant blue waters of the lake, making this a sporting paradise. Inside, the house is both spacious and gracious, with something of the feel of a baronial hunting lodge. Deep leather chairs, cushiony sofas, warm wood panelling and crackling fires set the tone, and dining here is a treat. Talented chef Tony Gudgin's seasonally changing menus take inspiration from the best of local produce and game from the estate. Outside, choose from a score of country pursuits, walk on wooded trails or simply soak up those views. There's even a Gothic tower on the lakeshore straight out of *Sleeping Beauty*. Fairytale indeed.

Love time	Bedrooms come replete with four-posters, private balconies, jacuzzi baths and every comfort – not to mention those intoxicating views.
Love bites	Bag a window table and, while feasting your eyes on those views, feast on confit of wild rabbit or roasted Vyrnwy estate lamb with couscous. Finish up with wickedly alcoholic caramelised pineapple soaked in tequila and lime.
Love it up	Lots of reasons (sigh) to get out of bed here: there's tennis, sailing, clay shooting, archery, trout fishing, birdwatching and more.
Who loves?	Lovebirds with a passion for the great outdoors.
You'll love ♥	Away-from-it-all lake and mountain vistas.

Penmaenuchaf Hall

Penmaenpool, Dolgellau
Gwynedd LL40 1YB
T 01341 422129
F 01341 422787
E relax@penhall.co.uk
W www.penhall.co.uk
Lorraine Fielding & Mark Watson

14 rooms
£125 to £185 per room per night
Dinner from £32.50

Open all year

From the A470: approaching Dolgellau take the A493 towards Tywyn and Fairbourne. The entrance to Penmaenuchaf is after 3/4 mile.

You can't beat the setting of this handsome Victorian mansion. This is location, location, location: Penmaenuchaf overlooks the Mawddach Estuary in the Snowdonia National Park, with to-die-for views all round, bounded by 20 acres of gardens ablaze with rhododendrons in springtime. The hotel has plenty of appeal inside, too. Beyond its heraldic crested entrance, a welcoming and tranquil haven awaits. Pleasing decor is set off by polished floors and wood panelling, oriental rugs and fresh flowers, plump sofas and deep armchairs. There's a richly decorated library stocked with books, and a rustic wooden hearth where logs burn merrily. Cosy up with a post-dinner chaser in the snug, or take your cue at the magnificent antique billiard table. Modern British cooking using the hotel's own garden-grown herbs is served in the oak-panelled dining room. A swing hangs from an old oak tree near the sunken rose garden outside – the perfect perch for taking in vistas of snow-laced mountains, wooded slopes and water.

Love time   Bedrooms glow in dusky pinks and yellows. One has an antique French double bed (ooh-la-la!) while others have four-posters, canopied beds or whirlpool baths. All have every amenity.

Love bites   It's a veritable local lovefest here: tuck into tender Welsh black beef, Bala lamb, wild trout from the Wnion and Celtic cheeses.

Love it up   Discover gold and slate mines, walk along empty beaches, take flight to the bird hide at Penmaenpool, go pony trekking or pedal off on bikes.

Who loves?   Guests report fabulous fun in the rooms with the jacuzzis. Now you know.

You'll love ♥   Old-time grandeur on a Welsh hillside.

WALES

St Tudno Hotel

North Parade, Promenade
Llandudno, Conwy LL30 2LP
T 01492 874411
F 01492 860407
E sttudnohotel@btinternet.com
W www.st-tudno.co.uk
Martin & Janette Bland

18 rooms, 2 suites
£105 to £220 per room per night
Dinner from £39.50

Open all year

From Chester: take the A55 for
Llandudno. Turn right at fifth roundabout
and follow signs for Promenade.
St Tudno is opposite the Pier entrance.

RR

Martin and Janette Bland's characterful hotel set in a prime position on Llandudno's famous promenade is a gem – and has all the awards to prove it. Continual upgrading over the years has retained the original Victorian feel, and reception areas enjoy period prettiness with great views over the sea. Bedrooms are beautifully decorated in pastels and patterned wallpapers, and most have whirlpool baths stocked with leading brand toiletries. Pace yourself for delectable Anglo-Welsh cuisine in the Italian style Terrace restaurant, complete with murals and a tented ceiling. It's not only acknowledged as one of the country's best kept tables but it's also a wine lover's paradise, with an outstanding 36-page list featuring great French vintages, rare medal-winning labels, boutique winery discoveries and well-selected house wines. Cheers to that. An indoor swimming pool and a secret garden complete the picture.

Love time   Sink into a double bathtub, splash each other with smellies, then slip on a monogrammed bathrobe or between Egyptian cotton sheets.

Love bites   Expect Welsh wizardry at the table. Head chef Stephen Duffy and his brigade have pulled in significant prizes for signature dishes such as Welsh black beef and hill lamb. There's superb seafood, too.

Love it up   Wales's natural beauty is the big draw here. Ride the narrow-gauge railway up Mount Snowdon, visit gardens and castles, go for a swim, or try dry-slope skiing and tobogganing.

Who loves?   Best-selling travel writer Bill Bryson raves about the food.

You'll love   Seaside pleasure par excellence.

Osborne House

17 North Parade, Promenade
Llandudno, Conwy LL30 2LP
T 01492 860330
F 01492 860791
E sales@osbornehouse.com
W www.osbornehouse.com
Elizabeth Maddocks

6 suites
£145 to £220 per room per night
Dinner from £25

Closed over Christmas

From Chester: take the A55 for
Llandudno. Turn right at
fifth roundabout and follow signs for
Promenade. Osborne House is
opposite the Pier. Staff will advise on
parking; let them know your ETA.

Imagine seaside holidays 150 years ago. The long carriage ride to the coast. The bathing machines. The constricting, formal clothes even in the height of summer. But then… the delicious, abundant food. The charming staff at your beck and call. The fireplaces in the bedrooms and the marble bathrooms. That's the beauty of Osborne House, a magnificently refurbished Victorian resort hotel that kisses the coast in the pretty town of Llandudno: you get all the style of bygone days, with none of the stuffiness. Owners Len and Elizabeth Maddocks whisked this 1851 seafront property from crumbling obscurity, lavished TLC on it, and have created a sparkling, all-suite townhouse. From the Prague crystal chandeliers to the antique Persian rugs, every detail is perfect and no expense has been spared.

Love time King-size brass beds in five of the suites are dressed with Egyptian cotton sheets, down duvets and feather pillows. Soak in style in marble bathrooms complete with clawfoot tubs.

Love bites The gloriously over-the-top restaurant (done out in theatrical black and gold, and lit by scores of candles) is the perfect place for dinner à deux. Nibble on pan-seared king scallops with a smoked salmon and rocket salad, or savour aromatic crispy duck and watercress with a piquant Thai dressing.

Love it up Visit nearby Portmeirion, setting for the cult TV series *The Prisoner*.

Who loves? Trendies tired of Chelsea and Brighton.

You'll love Extravagant Belle-Epoque style sure to make you weak at the knees.

WALES

The Old Rectory Country House

Llansanffraid, Glan Conwy
Conwy, Wales LL28 5LF
T 01492 580611
F 01492 584555
E info@oldrectorycountryhouse.co.uk
W www.oldrectorycountryhouse.co.uk
Wendy & Michael Vaughan

6 rooms
£119 to £169 per room per night
Dinner from £39.90

Closed 12 Dec – 12 Jan

From Chester: take the A55 to Llandudno, turning South onto the A470 (signed Betws-y-Coed) just before the town. The hotel is two miles from Llandudno Junction station.

The Welsh motto of this elegant Georgian country house painted in springtime daffodil yellow is Hardd Hafan Hedd, meaning beautiful haven of peace. It's soon apparent why: The Old Rectory harks back to a less hurried and calmer world. Hosts Wendy and Michael Vaughan more than deserve their accolade for Welsh Hospitality at its Best. Sympathetically restored in a charming but unfussy style, this supremely relaxing house is a pleasure to stay in. Watercolours, antiques, porcelain and a drawing room piano underline the sense of comfort, while thoroughly inviting bedrooms have lavishly draped four-poster or half-tester beds, cushiony sofas, well appointed bathrooms and goodies such as fresh fruit. Food lovers are in for a real treat here: Master Chef Wendy was the first woman in Wales to win a coveted Michelin star, and dinner starts with drinks in the panelled drawing room. Outside, terraced gardens tumble onto lawns stretching towards the water, with panoramic views of floodlit Conwy Castle and the River Conwy estuary. Snowdonia and the rugged Welsh coastline await discovery nearby.

Love time   Ask for the Mahogany room with its wonderful views of Conwy Castle and large corner bath for double soaking.

Love bites   Wendy's notable gastronomy includes monkfish with risotto or Welsh lamb with spinach parcels. At breakfast, it's Welsh rarebit – the real McCoy.

Love it up   Historic Conwy Castle and Snowdonia National Park cry out for exploration. Take flight to Conwy's bird sanctuary, or golf on a championship course.

Who loves?   Astronauts and aristocrats – they've all stayed here.

You'll love   A winner in the heart of Welsh Wales.

IRELAND

Go for the craic, Guinness and Irish jigs
Eat oysters, lobster and Dublin Bay prawns
Take your dancing shoes
Bedtime story? James Joyce: *The Dubliners*

145 • Letterkenny

A2 • Coleraine

144

• Derry ✈

A26 • Ballymena

A5

M2

A32

M2 ✈ • Belfast

• Donegal

N16 • Enniskillen

• Portadown

A1

• Sligo

146 • Monaghan

• Knock ✈

N4

147

173 • Clifden

171

172

N17

148

151 152 154

• Galway ✈ • Athlone

149 150 • Dublin ✈

153 157

170

155

N18

• Portlaoise

169

Carlow • N11

• Shannon ✈

• Limerick

158

167

168

N21

156

166

• Wexford

165 164

• Kerry ✈

N25 • Waterford

• Dingle

163

160

159

162 161

• Killarney

• Kenmare

• Cork ✈

N22

Pages 144-173

Bushmills Inn

9 Dunluce Road, Bushmills
Co. Antrim BT57 8QG
Northern Ireland
T 028 2073 2339
F 028 2073 2048
E mail@bushmillsinn.com
W www.bushmillsinn.com
Alan Dunlop & Stella Minogue

32 rooms
£98 to £248 per room per night
Dinner from £25

Open all year

From Derry: Take the A2 North directly to Bushmills. The Inn is right in the village, two miles from the Giant's Causeway
✈ Belfast, Derry

Let the tempestuous Atlantic waves crash on the rocks beneath craggy cliffs. Safe within the whitewashed walls of the Bushmills Inn, at the home of the world's oldest distillery, a leprechaun's hop away from the Giant's Causeway, the cosy light of welcome shines threefold. First the warmth of blazing turf fires, then the flicker of gaslight and finally the satisfying inner glow of a 25-year-old malt whiskey savoured in a rocking chair on old flagstones. Fortified against the seasons and the elements, find your room in the adjoining mill house on the banks of the River Bush. As eccentric and individual as the Inn, with its hidden tower library, bedrooms have comfy sitting areas and individual style. Perhaps you'll find an old fashioned slipper bath, maybe a four-poster or even, for the most intimate of rendezvous, a disappearing double bed, that by day folds away behind an innocent-seeming door and keeps your liaisons to itself.

Love time The 1608 suite with space to chase has a free-standing tub and huge bed.

Love bites The award-winning restaurant in the stables of this old coaching inn, with its whitewashed walls and cosy snugs, is the perfect place for an intimate dinner. Try the freshly-caught salmon and legendary sticky toffee pudding before retiring to the stove-fired loft with a rich Bushmills coffee – laced, naturally, with whiskey from the world's oldest distillery just up the road.

Love it up Clamber over the famous Giant's Causeway – a World Heritage site, and the centrepiece of Antrim's spectacular coastal scenery.

Who loves? A favourite haunt of TV presenters, writers and foodies.

You'll love ❯ Turf fires, flagstone floors and a tower where you'd happily be prisoners.

IRELAND

Rathmullan House

Lough Swilly, Rathmullan
Letterkenny, Co. Donegal
T +353 (0) 74 915 8188
F +353 (0) 74 915 8200
E info@rathmullanhouse.com
W www.rathmullanhouse.com
The Wheeler family

32 rooms
€176 to €297 per room per night
Dinner from €45

Closed Christmas

From Derry: take the A6 to Letterkenny, and R245 to Ramelton. Turn left at the bottom of the hill, cross the river and turn right by the bridge to Rathmullan (R247).
✈ Derry

Built in the 1760s as a summer house for Belfast bankers and run by the Wheeler family since 1963, Rathmullan retains all the graciousness of its grand history, hand-in-hand with a welcoming informality. Three warm and elegant sitting rooms replete with chandeliers, antiques, marble fireplaces and oil paintings are warmed by open turf fires in winter. Some bedrooms feature four-posters, others have balconies, while ground floor rooms have doors opening onto gardens filled with roses and cottage flowers. All offer the embracing comforts needed after a day of bracing Irish air. Outdoors, lawns and trees stretch down to two miles of deserted white sand beaches along the shores of Lough Swilly. Not up to a breezy dip? Relax in the indoor heated pool and steam room, or book a pampering aromatherapy massage.

Love time   Bask in the comfort of a luxury room, with a lounge area, lake views, patio or balcony.

Love bites   Donegal meets the desert here, and guests dine beneath an extravagant tented ceiling swathed in Bedouin silk. Menus are pure Ireland, using organic fruit and vegetables from the hotel's walled garden, locally caught seafood, and lamb grazed on the salt plains.

Love it up   Donegal's scenic coast and countryside share top honours here. Don't miss Glenveagh National Park and Glebe House, or spend a day at the Giant's Causeway and Bushmills whiskey distillery. Plenty of golfing, too.

Who loves?   Rathmullan has been billed a "honeymooner's delight."

You'll love ▸   De-stressing in delightful Donegal.

Castle Leslie

Glaslough, Co. Monaghan
T +353 (0) 47 88109
F +353 (0) 47 88256
E info@castleleslie.com
W www.castleleslie.com
Sammy Leslie

14 rooms
€250 to €350 per room per night
Dinner from €52

Open all year

From Armagh: take the A28 East, and turn onto the R185 to Glaslough after approx five miles.
✈ Dublin

Charismatic, fun and mildly eccentric, Castle Leslie is set within a rolling 1,000 acres overlooking Glaslough Lake. The owners claim to have descended from Attila the Hun, and later Leslies enjoyed a grand tour of Europe, where they acquired a vast collection of 16th and 17th century furniture. Crammed with Victoriana – be it stag's heads, family portraits, suits of armour or stuffed animals – the castle not surprisingly oozes history and interest. Rooms are done out in a flamboyant mix of antique furniture and deep colours. Play out your Jane Eyre fantasies in the Governess suite, ballroom dance your way across the huge painted bathroom in Anita's room or don your kimono for some eastern promise in the Chinese room. Downstairs is equally opulent, with elegant rooms lined with oil paintings and well-thumbed books. From one window you can see pastoral meadows and cattle, while from another, formal terraces stretch away behind curving balustrades.

Love time   Book the Mauve room, where royals galore have slumbered. Its thunderbox loo is aptly known as the Throne room.

Love bites   Dining is a relaxed affair with pre-dinner drinks in the drawing room or fountain garden depending on the season. Dinner (and the food's superb) is served in the original dining room, with its art-covered walls and candles.

Love it up   Tour the grounds on horseback, picnic on the lawns or fish for your supper in the lakes.

Who loves?   Rocker Paul McCartney tied the knot here with Heather Mills.

You'll love ❤   Blue-blooded setting for bedding down.

IRELAND

RⴲR

Ghan House

Carlingford, Co. Louth
T +353 (0) 42 937 3682
F +353 (0) 42 937 3772
E ghanhouse@eircom.net
W www.ghanhouse.com
Paul Carroll

11 rooms
€170 per room per night
Dinner from €47

Closed New Years Eve – 10 Jan

From Dublin: take the M1 to Dundalk and turn right onto the R173 to Carlingford. Ghan House is at the entrance to medieval Carlingford.
✈ Dublin, Belfast

Foodies make a beeline for Ghan House. Inspirational cooking has made it a hot ticket, and the setting – with views of Slieve Foy and the Mountains of Mourne – is the icing on the cake. Built in 1727, the house has heaps of history; it's surrounded by castellated towers and secret passageways. The interior stays true to period with bags of charm and comfort (log fires, family antiques and a tick-tock grandfather clock). Bedrooms are prettily done out and all have views. Chef Jeremy O'Connor's Michelin experience shines through in terrific staples like Carlingford mussels, oysters and lobster, Cooley organic beef, larders of game, homebakes and herbs from the garden. We pigged out on succulent panache of Gloucester old spot pork and melting, will-o-the-wisp Roquefort cheese soufflé. Want to get into the kitchen? The hotel even runs its own cookery courses and demos with guest chefs. Family owners the Carrolls encourage guests to have a high time of it, but this place is made for chilling, too.

Love time Slumber in a king-size or half-tester bed, in a room with a chaise longue, free-standing bath and views of the lough. That should do it.

Love bites Roll up for the full-on Georgian banquets or eight-course gourmet menu nights (with harpist) for the real works. Candlelit dining adds to the mood.

Love it up You're just a tree-length from Carlingford's medieval heritage: castles, the Mint, and a Dominican friary. Add to that walks in the Mourne Mountains, golf and sea sports, and you'll soon be whipping up an appetite.

Who loves? Townies, foodies and country gluttons looking to eat up and veg out.

You'll love ❦ A place that's game for a good time (even off the menu).

Wineport Lodge

Glasson, Athlone
Co. Westmeath
T +353 (0) 90 643 9010
F +353 (0) 90 648 5471
E lodge@wineport.ie
W www.wineport.ie
Ray Byrne & Jane English

10 rooms
€200 to €250 per room per night
Dinner from €55

Open all year

From Dublin: take the N4/N6 towards
Athlone and Galway. From the
Athlone ring road, take the N55 to
Ballykeeran. Fork left at the
Dog and Duck pub.
✈ Dublin

RR

This is officially a hideaway for wine lovers. However, with bubbly, hand-made chocs and fresh flowers in the VIP rooms, every taste is not only catered for but well and truly indulged. Wineport Lodge's waterside location reflects 1,500 years of wine arriving in Ireland from France, and its cellar reflects the best the world can offer. Room names – Taylors, Loire Valley, Tuscany and Jameson 1780 – evoke the great vintages savoured over dinner, and you can pick your mood music of choice from the CD racks in the double-height Taittinger lounge downstairs. All ten air-conditioned bedrooms have private balconies overlooking the lake, and flat-screen TVs for a change of scenery. Goose-down duvets, slippers and robes and toasty under-floor bathroom heating set a sensual tone. No worries about the pressures of everyday life lurking outside the bedroom door – top masseurs from Bliss Therapy are on hand to keep tension at bay for as long as you like.

Love time   Make it bath time here. Opt to soak in lavender body milk while sipping a Bailey's, or succumb to the froth and fizz combo of l'Occitane bath products and Bollinger.

Love bites   Chef Feargal O'Donnell blends classic techniques with regional ingredients, and his way with Dublin Bay prawns and prime Angus beef is a local legend. Upgrade your vice of choice to gluttony and order the carved rack of lamb for two, served with pesto mash and herb jus.

Love it up   Golf and shopping are just a few minutes away, but who needs to leave?

Who loves?   Bon vivants, and stars like Shirley Bassey.

You'll love ➤   Watching the sunset from your west-facing balcony.

IRELAND

Moyglare Manor

Maynooth, Co. Kildare
T +353 (0) 1 628 6351
F +353 (0) 1 628 5405
E info@moyglaremanor.ie
W www.moyglaremanor.ie
Shay Curran

15 rooms, 1 suite
€250 to €450 per room per night
Dinner from €55

Closed Christmas

From Dublin: take the M4 to Maynooth.
Moyglare Manor is located 1.5 miles past
the Roman Catholic church.
✈ Dublin

Ireland's Georgian buildings have a particular flourish and that's certainly the case in this imposing stone-built house deep in the heart of County Kildare's luscious greenery, with its woodlands and stud farms. It's approached through an avenue lined with tall trees and shrubs unfolding to reveal acres of pastures where some of the country's famous fillies graze. The house itself, classically simple on the outside, is extravagantly and gorgeously furnished with a profusion of fine antiques, drapes and plush wallpapers. Walls are bursting with portraits, mirrors and ornate lamps, while a log fire burns endlessly in the grate. The ambience is relaxed: this is Ireland, after all, and nothing here is stuffed apart from the armchairs. Bedrooms are spacious with high ceilings and – in many – four-poster or half-tester beds. Heavy chintz, velvets, silk rugs and large ensuite bathrooms exemplify a country house that's sweet as honey.

Love time   Sink into the Victorian splendour of Room One, with its ostentatious bathroom and canopied bath.

Love bites   Deep pink walls and clusters of candelabra set the scene for award-winning cuisine, which includes produce fresh that day from the hotel's gardens and orchards. And you'll want more than a drop from the famous Moyglare vintage cellars.

Love it up   Horse racing, golf and country walks are on the doorstep, while you're only 18 miles from the urban delights of Dublin.

Who loves?   Shameless romantics.

You'll love ❤   Irish charm and twinkle on a grand scale.

The Clarence

6-8 Wellington Quay, Dublin 2
T +353 (0) 1 407 0800
F +353 (0) 1 407 0820
E reservations@theclarence.ie
W www.theclarence.ie
Robert Van Eerde

43 rooms, 5 suites
€315 to €2100 per room per night
Dinner from €50

Open all year

From city centre (O'Connell Street):
follow one-way system into
Westmoreland Street, and turn left
into the Quays just before
O'Connell Bridge.
✈ Dublin

When Bono and The Edge bought up the Clarence, its fans were unsure what to expect. But the renaissance is fabulous; things are truly spiffy by the Liffey. The refurb has stayed true to the restrained Arts and Crafts interior and married it cleverly with modernism. Public areas retain the oak panelling, stone floors and bronze-framed windows, while furniture has Art Nouveau and simple Shaker influences. But this clean-limbed simplicity is deceptive – the mood here is decidedly sybaritic. Individually designed bedrooms preen in rich crimson, gold and amethyst fabrics, set off with nickel-plated period desk lamps, and candle sconces with coloured glass diffusers. Rooms also boast up-to-the-minute digital interactive entertainment systems, and there's a stellar duplex penthouse on the top floor with to-die-for views. Chef Anthony Ely's award-winning menu in the airy Tea Room restaurant – the former ballroom – isn't to be quickly waltzed through. Then there are the pampering treatments: an Air Walk or Zeus Boost, anyone? The hotel's in the heart of the riverfront; a microcosm of sophisticated Dublin. Rock on Clarence.

Love time   The loft-style duplex Penthouse is a wow, complete with a baby grand piano, wrap-around roof terrace and outdoor hot tub – plus, plus, plush.

Love bites   The soaring Tea Room restaurant serves critically acclaimed new wave Irish food. Try the deep-fried bacon potato cakes – peasant's perfection.

Love it up   You're on Dublin's Left Bank near the hot and happening Temple Bar district. The city's at your feet.

Who loves?   Rock music legends U2, and more.

You'll love ▸ Pop meets papal here in one of the coolest places to stay.

IRELAND

Number 31

31 Leeson Close
Lower Leeson Street, Dublin 2
T +353 (0) 1 676 5011
F +353 (0) 1 676 2929
E info@number31.ie
W www.number31.ie
Noel Comer

20 rooms
€120 to €240 per room per night

Open all year

From city centre: Leeson Close
is behind Fitzwilliam Place, off
Lower Leeson Street.
✈ Dublin

Things have gone groovy in the heart of Georgian Dublin. Look for the ivy-covered wall and discreet brass plate down a quiet side street, press the button and hey, presto. You're in another world. This totally chilled mews-style residence (actually it's two 19th century coach houses) reached via a private courtyard is one of the best little finds in Ireland. Friendly owners Noel and Deirdre Comer (dog Homer is also there to meet and greet) call this place a B&B. We'd say it feels more like a little boutique hideaway. Clock the sunken lounge with its mosaic floor, modern art, open fire and leather sofas on the way in. The building was designed by top Irish architect Sam Stephenson and the Comers have kept its spacious, open-plan feel. No two rooms are the same. Walls are cream or white with fabrics, wood and stone contrasting stylishly against cool, clean lines. Oriental rugs and original art are strewn around, and some rooms have private patios. There's a spirit of fun and bonhomie about the place, epitomised by the sunny conservatory, where breakfast is served family style. Definitely worth getting out of bed for.

Love time — Bag a Superior room for the max in space and comfort.
Love bites — Breakfast is a not-to-be-missed affair. Delicious eats include mushroom frittata and freshly baked cranberry and walnut bread. Your hosts will suggest some good spots for dinner.
Love it up — Dublin awaits outside the door: you're minutes from St Stephen's Green, Trinity College and Temple Bar.
Who loves? — You'd be surprised. This is an Irish home-from-home for a top US senator.

You'll love ❤ — More luxe for less: cool surroundings, great value.

The Morrison

Ormond Quay, Dublin 1
T +353 (0) 1 887 2400
F +353 (0) 1 878 3185
E info@morrisonhotel.ie
W www.morrisonhotel.ie
Andrew O'Neill

83 rooms, 7 suites
€285 to €1,450 per room per night
Dinner from €35

Open all year

The hotel is five minutes from the city centre and a €25 taxi ride from Dublin Airport.
✈ Dublin

🛏 🔔 RR

Fashion supremo John Rocha and Irish designer Douglas Wallace have created a temple of benchmark modernism behind the facade of an 18th century townhouse here beside the Liffey. High ceilings and polished stone floors top and tail gleaming white walls. Accents are provided by grey hand-crafted carpets and original art by Clea van der Gryn. Bedroom decor is soothingly monochromatic; a palette of blacks, chocolates and creams with a splash of vibrant colour provided by velvet throws. Sheets are by Frette, baths have limestone floors, walk-in showers and double sinks, and there's every bit of techno wizardry going. In Halo, the dramatically designed split-level restaurant with its hundred foot high ceiling and huge triptych, guests can rub shoulders with Dublin's glitterati while heaping praise on Jean-Michel Poulot's innovative oriental and classical French cuisine. Lobo, the late-night bar, mixes a mean cocktail and keeps the crowd chilled. It's hip and happening, and the staff positively encourage you to have fun.

Love time   The secluded Penthouse boasts a giant jacuzzi, steamroom and sauna, a double-sided TV visible from both bath and bed, state-of-the-art sound and views over the Liffey.

Love bites   Dramatic Halo dazzles with wicked cuisine; the Café Bar lays on terrific brunches while the Lobo lounge bar pumps into the small hours.

Love it up   You're close to the city's hotspots here, and two minutes' walk from the buzzy Temple Bar quarter.

Who loves?   Fashionistas, boy bands and trendies.

You'll love ▸   Where Dublin's dubbed uber-cool.

IRELAND

Brownes Hotel & Restaurant

22 St Stephen's Green, Dublin 2
T +353 (0) 1 638 3939
F +353 (0) 1 638 3900
E info@brownesdublin.com
W www.brownesdublin.com
Sonia Santana

10 rooms, 1 suite
€175 to €375 per room per night
Dinner from €60

Closed Christmas and New Year

The hotel is a 20-minute cab ride from both Dublin Airport and the main rail station.
✈ Dublin

🛏 🔔 RR

Overlooking leafy St Stephen's Green – Dublin's oldest square – Brownes is a regular stop-off for visiting celebs. One of *the* places to stay in this spirited city, it's a ravishing Georgian townhouse hotel in a top-notch location, whose lavishly decorated rooms are designed to seduce. Brownes clinched the title of best newcomer hotel and restaurant in the British Isles in 2003, and you'll soon see why. Decor throughout is a mix of soft creams, rich chocolate and deep red, with open fires, vases of flowers, gilded mirrors, chandeliers and heavy drapes adding to the sense of luxury. Magnificent suites include the Lord Shelbourne, with its four-poster, antique furnishings and gold leaf ceiling. Wickedly romantic Brownes restaurant, with its plush velvet banquettes and hideaway corners, has become an evening destination in its own right. Lovebirds make a beeline for the honeymooner's table, designed for cornerside cooing and wooing. Ready to surface? Dublin's fair city is on the doorstep.

Love time   Play out your movie star fantasies in glamorous suites designed for lurve. Big beds, thick walls and champagne on call. You want more?

Love bites   Continental dishes with a zest of new Irish cuisine are the hallmarks of chef Raymond Heekpo's contemporary menus. How does chargrilled halibut with pommes écrasées, aubergine caviar and fish velouté sound?

Love it up   Brownes is just steps away from the shopping mecca of Grafton Street. You're also close to Trinity College and myriad museums and galleries.

Who loves?   Plenty of A-listers including the McCartneys.

You'll love ▸   A sumptuous Dublin delight.

Belcamp Hutchinson

Balgriffin, Dublin 17
T +353 (0) 1 846 0843
F +353 (0) 1 848 5703
E belcamphutchinson@eircom.net
W www.belcamphutchinson.com
Doreen Gleeson

8 rooms
€140 per room per night

Closed Christmas and New Year

From Dublin Airport: head towards
city centre and turn left onto the M50
at first roundabout. Turn left towards
Malahide at first major junction,
then left just after Campions pub.
✈ Dublin

Jetting off on honeymoon? Forget soulless airport hotels, and check in here – you may just decide to stay for your entire holiday. Although it's just 15 minutes from the centre of Dublin, this elegant country house B&B simply exudes rural charm. It was originally a family home, and with only eight bedrooms, will make you feel like honoured – and very fortunate – friends, especially as your hostess Doreen makes a point of introducing you to your fellow guests. Within the ivy-clad walls, the interior glows with good taste. Graciously proportioned rooms, ornate decor, fresh flowers and gleaming woodwork take you back to the house's leisurely Georgian past, and every comfort is laid on, even down to bottles of scent on your bedside table. Outside, there are four acres of gardens for you to explore, and a circular maze. Don't worry about getting lost – Digger, Dusty and Lady, the three resident dogs, are there for walkies.

Love time   Individually styled bedrooms range from the exotic Gold room, with its sumptuous brass bed, to the cream walled, patchwork-quilted Wicker room. All come complete with candles and choccies.

Love bites   Share a generous Irish breakfast in the dining room (traditionalists will relish the real porridge, eggs and bacon; while others can nibble a croissant or stock up on vitamins with a bowl of berries). For dinner, explore a host of excellent restaurants.

Love it up   Nearby Malahide village is great for retail therapy, and there's golf aplenty.
Who loves?   Couples after a hideaway that's chic, intimate and ultra-convenient.

You'll love Irish eyes are smiling at this friendly rural address.

IRELAND

Clone House

Aughrim, Co. Wicklow
T +353 (0) 402 36121
F +353 (0) 402 36029
E stay@clonehouse.com
W www.clonehouse.com
Carla Edigati Watson

7 rooms
€120 to €180 per room per night
Dinner from €49.50

Open all year

From Dublin: take the M11 South to Rathnew, then the R752 to Aughrim and follow the brown tourist signs to the hotel.
✈ Dublin

Here's a treat. Lovers of Ireland and Italy bag both worlds at Clone House, an hour South of Dublin. This elegantly appointed Georgian house with rustic touches is deep in Wicklow's Aughrim Hills, set in its own pretty garden with waterfall and ponds. Owners are the Watsons; Jeff is green-fingered (the evidence is all around) and Carla, from Tuscany, loves her cooking (as will you). Many ingredients come from their organically nurtured herb and vegetable plots. The three and five-course dinner menu marries Emerald Isle with Med – so expect dishes like mascarpone and spinach gnocchi, chicken with Parma ham and porcini, focaccia alongside soda bread and virgin oils aplenty. Wines include many Italian faves. Buon appetito! Fall contentedly into a king-size four-poster in a pretty room warmed by a real fire, and go for the full Irish next morning with some of Carla's continental bakeries. Work it off later in the little gym, stroll the grounds or plonk yourself down by the stone hearth in the music room with a paper and a coffee. Life in Clone House is as lazy or exerting as you want it, and in every way simpatico.

Love time Richly decorated Vale of Aroca has a skylight right above the bed. Snuggle down and share the secrets of the stars.
Love bites Chef Carla reveals her native roots with Tuscan influenced cuisine; densely flavoured ossobuco, risotto, home-made pasta and glorious oils.
Love it up Walk along the Wicklow Way and sand-duned Brittas Beach, swim or play golf, visit historic houses, or try Angling For All (catch guaranteed).
Who loves? Dreamers, foodies, country lovers and Italophiles.

You'll love ❧ Where Ireland goes un poco italiano.

Cullintra House

The Rower, Inistioge
Co. Kilkenny
T +353 (0) 51 423614
E cullhse@indigo.ie
W http://indigo.ie/~cullhse/
Patricia Cantlon

6 rooms
€60 to €90 per room per night
Dinner €35

Open all year

From Dublin: take the N7/M7 to
Newbridge, then the M9/N9 past
Carlow, and turn onto the R705.
Cullintra House is signed
along this road.
✈ Waterford, Dublin

If you've been saving that special bottle of wine, take it with you to the whimsical and special Cullintra House. That's just one of the many quirks and delights of staying with the lively and free-spirited Patricia Cantlon, artist, prize-winning chef, acclaimed flower arranger and mentor of Libby-Muffin, Oswald, Penelope-Jane and several other felines. Guests bring their own wines to the table to accompany a magical and long-drawn-out meal. Be prepared to dine late and sleep late too, since early-to-rise is not the way things are done in this delightfully relaxed, ivy-covered farmhouse set amid 230 acres of meadows and woodland at the foot of Mount Brandon. Relax with tea or coffee in the airy studio conservatory, or cosy up by the log fire before retiring. Patricia is something of a night owl, and you can call to reserve a room until two in the morning. Some bedrooms are ensuite, and guests are asked to stay a minimum of two nights.

Love time Comfortable bedrooms – some in the converted stables and barn – have flair and originality.

Love bites Patricia is an excellent cook and the five-course candlelit dinner with delicious mains, Irish cheeses and a choice of desserts is worth waiting for. Breakfast, served on locally made pottery, is a late and lazy affair and it's not unusual to be at the table here until midday.

Love it up Wander with wildlife and explore. Take a private pathway to nearby Brandon Hill and the 4,000 year old cairn.

Who loves? All types! Cat lovers especially welcome.

You'll love ☞ The informality of a hideaway where time has no place.

IRELAND

Hunter's Hotel

Newrath Bridge
Rathnew, Co. Wicklow
T +353 (0) 404 40106
F +353 (0) 404 40338
E reception@hunters.ie
W www.hunters.ie
The Gelletlie family

16 rooms
€90 to €100 per person per night
Dinner from €40

Closed Christmas

From Dublin: Take the N11 for Rathnew.
Just before Rathnew take the R761 to
the left, signed Newcastle. The hotel
is one kilometre down this road.
✈ Dublin

It's easy to imagine anguished poets scribbling love sonnets and the odd billet doux in the gardens of this 300-year-old former coaching inn on the banks of the River Varty, so sublime is the setting. An Emerald Isle gem, Hunter's has romance written all over it. Owned and run by the Gelletlie family since 1825, this mellow stone-built house resonates with charm. Brass glints by the fireside, old wood glows, clocks tick and turf bricks sizzle in the hearth. In short, it's the kind of hideaway you'd like to hole up in for days. Cross the tiled entrance hall, with its creaky staircase and grandfather clock, and cradle a whiskey ensconced in an old-fashioned armchair in the bar, or take tea in the elegant drawing room. Bedrooms gleam with antiques and freshly-painted wood, while jugs of fresh flowers help make the pretty yellow dining room a treat. The gardens themselves – a riot of rhododendrons, tulips, magnolias and the fronds of palm trees – are the cherry on the cake here. Meander along the riverside walk, linger over a pre-dinner drink by the lawn or just soak up the scents of a myriad flowers.

Love time — Top-floor rooms above the gardens offer the max in seclusion and views.

Love bites — Dinners are a four-course affair on tables decked in crisp linen and silver. Hearty fare might include rack of Wicklow lamb, Dublin Bay crab and wicked white chocolate mousse.

Love it up — County Wicklow is the Garden of Ireland, so check out the grounds of Powerscourt, Mount Usher, Russborough House and Glendalough.

Who loves? — Romantic royals: regulars include Sweden's King Carl Gustav and his queen.

You'll love ❦ — An Irish hideaway worth running away to.

Kilgraney House

Bagenalstown, Co. Carlow
T +353 (0) 59 977 5283
F +353 (0) 59 977 5595
E info@kilgraneyhouse.com
W www.kilgraneyhouse.com
Bryan Leech

6 rooms, 2 suites
€90 to €170 per room per night
Dinner from €45

Closed mid Nov – end Feb

From Dublin: take the N7/M7, then the M9/N9. After Carlow, join the R705. The hotel is halfway between Bagenalstown and Borris, just off this road.
✈ Dublin

From the outside Kilgraney looks every bit your typical Georgian house, but cross the threshold and you're thrown a few left curves. True, there are those classic antiques but what's this? Some tall and curvy Marilyn chairs, artefacts made from coconut shells, intriguing ethnic art, and light pulls made from lovespoons or tasselled walking sticks. These are just some of the characterful design moves pulled off with flair and no little irony by owners Bryan Leech and Martin Marley. The hotel's idiosyncratic style is a charmer. Chic bedrooms are individually done up with lush exotic touches, and guests gather convivially around a communal table in the cherub-adorned dining room at night. The six-course menu is modern and inspired, with many ingredients grown in the grounds. And those grounds unfurl with myriad pleasures: discover woodland and aromatic herbal tea walks, a medieval herb courtyard, orchards and monastic cloisters. A new therapeutic spa is just the place for more unwinding with pampering herbal treatments. Herbs are big here: in fact, Kilgraney does wonders for one's karma.

Love time   Travel the globe here at night – sleep in tasteful Thai, serene Buddha or wicked zebra skin surrounds.
Love bites   Dine à deux or in company. Signature dishes include home-smoked duck and noodle salad, or wild Slaney salmon wrapped in nori and wasabi.
Love it up   Chill in the outdoor tub, walk the South Leinster Way, visit Altamont gardens, check out medieval Kilkenny, or get sporty.
Who loves?   Townies who love their country quirky.

You'll love ❥   The double take. Straight-laced Georgian outside, fabulously eclectic inside.

Dunbrody House

Arthurstown, New Ross
Co. Wexford
T +353 (0) 51 389600
F +353 (0) 51 389601
E dunbrody@indigo.ie
W www.dunbrodyhouse.com
Kevin & Catherine Dundon

14 rooms, 7 suites
€200 to €400 per room per night
Dinner from €55

Closed 20-26 Dec

From Dublin: take the N11 and R733 to
Arthurstown. From Cork: take the N25
to Waterford and Passage East
car ferry to Ballyhack.
✈ Cork

What's cooking? Rather a lot. This is one of the more luscious slices of County Wexford, and Dunbrody, ringed by neat lawns and parkland on a dramatic peninsula, makes a terrific starter. Let's approach some mains. It's an impressive, mellow Regency house, sometime family seat of the Marquis of Donegal, whose decor effortlessly marries lordly Georgian with contemporary swish. Spacious bedrooms are garnished with gorgeous looks, garden views, a terrific spa and top-notch bathrooms. Dunbrody's owned by acclaimed Master Chef Kevin Dundon and his wife, Catherine. The icing on the cake is the dedicated cookery school beside the house. Kevin's philosophy allows guests at any level to hone their skills avoiding needlessly complex recipes and methods. However, you can enjoy life here without tussling pots and pans. Take a seat in the stylish dining room, with its dark walls, modern art and sculptural long-stemmed blooms. We relished our pinky-perfect Barbary duck with burnt orange sauce, the jus densely flavoured. This is definitely the place for bons vivants – which leaves only one course open to you.

Love time How about the sleigh bed? And after gourmandising the night before it has to be the champagne breakfast in bed.

Love bites Aside from enjoying Kevin Dundon's masterful cuisine, guests can learn from him in the adjoining cookery school (and become half as good!).

Love it up Try out the hotel's swanky new spa, craft-and-crystal shop in Wexford and Waterford, go walking or swing out on championship courses.

Who loves? Mary McAleese, President of Ireland, stays. So do big and little piggies.

You'll love ❥ Coming here to blissfully trough and cook.

Longueville House

Mallow, Co. Cork
T +353 (0) 22 47156
F +353 (0) 22 47459
E info@longuevillehouse.ie
W www.longuevillehouse.ie
Aisling O'Callaghan

20 rooms
€180 to €360 per room per night
Dinner from €55

Closed Christmas and second half Feb

From Cork: take the N20 to Mallow, then turn left onto the N72 signed Killarney. Take the right hand turn to Ballyclough after a few miles.

✈ Cork

Longueville resonates with history and a return to grand Ireland. This 500-acre estate has seen off 17th century rebellions, forfeiture by Oliver Cromwell and has oak trees dating back to the Battle of Waterloo. With its wooded grounds, walled garden, Smoke Walk (where gentlemen used to puff on their cigars after dinner) and fairytale views of a leprechaun-green river valley and castle, it has all the feel of a grandly leisured age. Decorative ceilings, an Adams fireplace, statement-making staircase and inlaid mahogany doors all add refinement to the Georgian setting. There's also a stunning circular Victorian conservatory, pretty-pretty under candlelight. Chef-patron William O'Callaghan (whose family have owned Longueville on and off for centuries) tempts with flair and with fare from the estate's gardens, farms and rivers. You'll get a glass of fizz before dinner (and tea when you arrive). Traditionally decorated bedrooms – all velvets, florals and pastels – look gorgeous and feel gorgeous at this dreamily out-of-time manor house.

Love time   The Vineyard suite has to be the pick of the bunch. Other rooms look kissably pretty with classic design and lush furnishings.

Love bites   Ochre walls, flickering candles and silver service mark out the President's restaurant – the heart of the house – as splendidly special. Owner and chef William O'Callaghan governs here with gourmet authority.

Love it up   Cycle or wander through the grounds, go fly-fishing on the estate (William will cook your catch), join game and clay pigeon shoots, or go golfing.

Who loves?   Sophisticates after sporting splendour.

You'll love ❧   A grand manor that's Longue on comforts.

IRELAND

Ard na Sidhe

Caragh Lake, Killarney
Co. Kerry
T +353 (0) 66 976 9105
F +353 (0) 64 71350
E sales@kih.liebherr.com
W www.killarneyhotels.ie
Aidan O'Sullivan

18 rooms
€150 to €270 per room per night
Dinner from €50

Closed 30 Sept – 1 May

From Killarney: take the N72 to Killorglin. Continue on the N70 for five miles then turn left for Caragh Lake. Once in Caragh village, follow signs to the hotel.
✈ Kerry

The name in Gaelic means Hill of the Fairies, and if that sounds a tad too whimsical just wait till you see its magical position overlooking Caragh Lake in the foothills of Ireland's highest mountain range, the McGillicuddy Reeks. If that's not pleasure enough there are award-winning gardens where paths wind down to the tranquil lakeshore through giant ferns, azaleas, rhododendrons and magnolias. Built in 1913, the ivy-clad house follows the spell cast by the scenery; it's a handsome Victorian edifice with many features elegantly intact, and a smaller garden house alongside. Both are filled with antique furnishings and paintings, and bedrooms don't stint on those views. Enjoy a whiskey on the terrace and wallow in the stillness on a balmy summer evening before being seated for dinner in the intimate dining room, where dishes (which thankfully don't come fairy-sized) combine modern Irish cooking with international specialities. Many guests report how much they enjoy the mystical atmosphere here – and we don't think they're off with the fairies.

Love time   Classically furnished bedrooms offer space and fairytale lake views.
Love bites   Traditional favourites here include duck with blackcurrant sauce, avocado and shrimp salad and scrummy Black Forest gateau.
Love it up   Take to the lake: row to your heart's content or trawl for a catch in the hotel's own boat. Enjoy complimentary use of the leisure centres at two sister properties, play golf or discover the scenic Ring of Kerry.
Who loves?   Would-be Sir Galahads and their ladies.

You'll love ❥ A grand taste of Irish country living.

Carrig House

Caragh Lake, Killorglin, Co. Kerry
T +353 (0) 66 976 9100
F +353 (0) 66 976 9166
E info@carrighouse.com
W www.carrighouse.com
Frank & Mary Slattery

16 rooms
€130 to €350 per room per night
Dinner from €40

Closed Dec – Feb

From Tralee: take the N70 to Killorglin, and continue towards Glenbeigh on the main Ring of Kerry road. Turn left after 2.5 miles for Caragh Lake.
✈ Kerry

Old world Irish hospitality and charm are the essence of this delightful antique-yellow Victorian country house on the shores of Caragh Lake. Tucked into a sheltered lakeside dell with a carpet of moss and ferny glades, the four-acre gardens are ablaze with colour in spring and summer, when azaleas and camellias are in full bloom. Leafy acers add flourishes of copper and gold in autumn. The hotel's comfortable drawing rooms, with their polished floors, rugs and open turf fires, are a picture of cosy serenity. William Morris style wallpapers, crisp white linen and gleaming glassware set the tone in the dining room, where huge bay windows frame spectacular lake views. Bedrooms too, individually decorated with antique furniture, look out across the lake to the wild Kerry mountains beyond. Likeable hosts Frank and Mary Slattery encourage guests to mingle, though you might decide this is just the place to slip upstairs unseen.

Love time   Plump for exotic Room 12, with its gold wallpaper, plum-coloured raw silk curtains and hand-painted antique Italian bed. Or splash out on the huge Presidential suite, with its jacuzzi bath and the best views in Ireland.

Love bites   How about black and white seafood pudding on Carrageen moss with saffron vinaigrette? Locally sourced ingredients help create an inspired range of dishes, including vegetarian, in the critically acclaimed restaurant.

Love it up   This is a place for golf, sailing, horse riding, hillwalking and watersports. Don't miss a day's drive around the Ring of Kerry and Dingle Peninsula.

Who loves?   Actors, ambassadors and pop icons.

You'll love ▸   Echoes of another era in this gracious lakeside manor.

Caragh Lodge

Caragh Lake, Killorglin, Co. Kerry
T +353 (0) 66 976 9115
F +353 (0) 66 976 9316
E caraghl@iol.ie
W www.caraghlodge.com
Mary & Graham Gaunt

14 rooms, 1 suite
€140 to €350 per room per night
Dinner from €45

Closed 17 Oct – 21 Apr

From Killorglin: take the N70 towards Glenbeigh and take the second road, signed Caragh Lodge 1 mile. Turn left at the lake and the hotel is on your right.

✈ Kerry

The setting's a stunner: green lawns sweeping down to the dazzling waters of Lake Caragh with the lofty McGillicuddy Reeks rising up beyond. This mid-Victorian former fishing lodge is certainly a dream for those who dig their gardens: Caragh Lodge is wrapped in seven acres of flowering rhododendrons, magnolias, azaleas, rare sub-tropical plants and towering Scotch pines. It's also for people who love digging into great food. Owner and chef Mary Gaunt delivers here with a flourish. That means prime Kerry lamb, succulent seafood, garden-grown veg, freshly-baked breads, delicious breakfasts and home-made treats for afternoon tea. What's more, the elegant, clubby dining room with its warming fire has terrific views of the lake and gardens. Salons have sink-right-in comforts and turf fires, while bedrooms are furnished with antiques and softest touches. Caragh is also for people who hanker after having the wind in their hair in Ireland's finest landscape, whether mountain, shore or lake.

Love time   Garden rooms all have period prettiness, and the scent of flowers right outside the window.

Love bites   Ooh-aah dishes include Dover sole with champagne sauce, crispy half-roast duck with plum sauce, and toothsome sticky toffee pudding.

Love it up   Go golfing (championship and parkland courses abound), take to the lake in the hotel's own boats, swim on Dingle's beaches or fish for salmon and trout. Kerry's spectacular mountain country begs exploration.

Who loves?   Foodies and fans of Ireland in bloom.

You'll love ❤   Lakeside flower power in full pelt.

Emlagh House

Dingle, Co. Kerry
T +353 (0) 66 9152345
F +353 (0) 66 9152369
E info@emlaghhouse.com
W www.emlaghhouse.com
The Kavanagh family

10 rooms
€160 to €260 per room per night

Closed Nov – mid Mar

From Tralee: take the N86 to Dingle.
The hotel is a few minutes from
the town centre.
✈ Kerry

Built a few years ago in pleasingly traditional style, Emlagh House looks every bit the old-time country house. Grand period furniture and pretty landscaped gardens are matched by every modern comfort. Help yourself to a drink from the honesty bar in the drawing room – a real place to escape from it all with an open fire, views over the garden and harbour, games and a piano. There's a library with internet access on the first floor and a great collection of books on local history. Breakfast is served in the sunny conservatory with its stripped wood floors, stylish seating and wide-open views over the harbour (keep an eye out for Fungi, the resident dolphin). Native wild Irish flowers were the inspiration behind the colour-themed bedrooms, four of which have their own private patio. All are designed to please with CD players, good lighting, lush linens and comfy down duvets, not to mention deep baths with marble surrounds.

Love time   The Fuschia room is a riot of red, gold, purple and black with a half-tester bed and red sofa – perfect for passion.

Love bites   Breakfast here is a full three-course feast: look forward to smoked salmon and scrambled eggs, home-baked soda bread and scones. Dingle's score of restaurants and bars offer plenty of evening options.

Love it up   This is a great base for exploring the wild beauty and white sand beaches of the Dingle peninsula. Riding, deepsea fishing and golf are on the doorstep, and you're minutes from Dingle town centre.

Who loves?   Outdoor lovers who cherish their creature comforts.

You'll love ♥   The smart place to stay in cosmopolitan Dingle.

Gorman's Clifftop House

Glaise Bheag, Ballydavid
Dingle Peninsula, Co. Kerry
T +353 (0) 66 9155162
F +353 (0) 66 9155003
E info@gormans-clifftophouse.com
W www.gormans-clifftophouse.com
Sile & Vincent Gorman

7 rooms, 2 suites
€130 to €170 per room per night
Dinner from €35

Open all year
(Nov – Mar by reservation only)

From Dingle: drive through town with sea
on left to roundabout West of town.
Follow sign marked An Fheothanach and
drive for eight miles. Keep left.
✈ Kerry

🌳 🐋 🛏 ♿ ✳

RR

Heading West takes on a whole new meaning at Gorman's, set in the furthest reaches of south-west Ireland on one of the loveliest stretches of coastline imaginable. Owners Vincent and Sile Gorman have transformed this snug hotel on the Dingle peninsula from a simple B&B into something rather special. Elegant, traditionally furnished rooms gaze out over the Atlantic while the restaurant, looking across Smerwick harbour and the Three Sisters, comes into its own after dark. Right at the heart of this very traditional corner of Ireland where Gaelic is still spoken, the house matches simplicity with comfort, with rustic pine furniture, open fires, hand-thrown pottery lamps and tapestries. Outside, the huge skies, deserted shores and dramatic Brandon mountains just beg to be shared. Long sandy beaches lead to little coves and tucked-away harbours, while ever-changing light and cloud formations bring nature up close. Room service is on call from eight till late indoors, positively encouraging lovers to stay lazily under the sheets.

Love time View the sun setting over the Atlantic from your bedroom window, where spray from the sea below lashes the windows on stormy nights, or make waves of your own in a deep jacuzzi bathtub.

Love bites Vincent takes his cooking seriously. Tuck into delicious Dingle Bay prawns and crab claws, followed by tender Irish beef and farmyard cheeses.

Love it up Take one of the hotel's bikes for a ride along Slea Head Drive or find a craggy suntrap on the beach to watch the crashing waves.

Who loves? Outdoor romantics with a passion for sea and sky.

You'll love ❥ Cocooning comfort next to the tang of the ocean waves.

Ballygarry House

Killarney Road, Tralee, Co. Kerry
T +353 (0) 66 712 3322
F +353 (0) 66 712 7630
E info@ballygarryhouse.com
W www.ballygarryhouse.com
Padraig McGillicuddy

38 rooms, 8 suites
€190 to €260 per room per night
Dinner from €35

Closed Christmas and two weeks Jan

From Dublin: take the N7 to Limerick, then the N21 to Tralee.
✈ Kerry

You'll feel right at home at Ballygarry. This hospitable family-run hotel in Ireland's south-west corner, set in six acres of tended gardens at the foot of the Kerry Mountains, is on the doorstep of a score of scenic beauty spots. It's a pleasure inside, too: impeccably furnished, with fresh-cut flowers, the friendliest staff (you really get the feeling nothing's too much trouble here) and inviting open fires. Spacious, individually designed rooms are traditionally furnished, with well co-ordinated colours and fabrics. Downstairs, it's just the place for making yourself at home. Bask in the glow of a turf fire in the library – the perfect spot for sinking a creamy Irish coffee – or enjoy drinks beneath sheltering garden trees in summer. Just as enticing is the hotel's setting; this is the place to get your fill of lakes, mountains and seashore. Golfers are spoiled for choice in this greener than green corner of Ireland (truly the Emerald Isle), whose finest fairways are on the doorstep.

Love time   Bedrooms have lashings of space, cushion-strewn sofas and springy carpets. Expect fluffy robes and a good stock of pampering lotions.

Love bites   All is light and fresh in the pillared, split-level dining room, where guests dine on the likes of Atlantic oysters, rack of Kerry lamb on wilted greens and a port and thyme jus, or pepper-crusted yellowfin tuna.

Love it up   Scenery here is top-drawer. Choose from the Dingle peninsula's wild, rocky bays and Atlantic beaches; Ireland's loftiest peaks (at times snow-capped) in the Ring of Kerry; and hillsides splashed with foxgloves and fuschia.

Who loves?   Top names from the golfing fraternity have holed up here.

You'll love ❤   Having good reasons to stay in (great bedrooms) and go out (great golf).

IRELAND

Glin Castle

Glin, Co. Limerick
T +353 (0) 68 34173
F +353 (0) 68 34364
E knight@iol.ie
W www.glincastle.com
Bob Duff

15 rooms
€275 to €440 per room per night
Dinner from €47

Closed end Nov – 1 March

From Shannon: Follow signs for Cork and Limerick, then take N69 for 32 miles. Turn left into Glin village and right at top of the square.
✈ Shannon, Kerry

This castellated 18th century Georgian Gothic fortress is the ancestral seat of Desmond FitzGerald, 29th Knight of Glin, and his wife Madam Olda. The setting's grand: a 500 acre domain on the Shannon estuary with fabulous gardens, a series of follies and avenues of trees. Swooning already? Wait till you get inside. There are acres of inherited antiques and family portraits – all top notch – set against fine architectural detailing that includes Corinthian pillars, Adams ceilings and neo-classical embellishments. The elegance extends into lavishly decorated bedrooms, all with their own individual character and more period pieces. The formal dining room boasts various ancient portraits of former knights who weren't fortunate enough to enjoy chef Lionel Luis's delicious Irish country-house cuisine, using ingredients grown on the estate. Weddings are held here with style. Staff are delightful and your hosts (who sometimes join their guests) are delightfully unfuddy-duddy. Here's a chance to hang your hat in a stately home that's absolutely the real McCoy.

Love time   Lay claim to the Yellow Crown room, with its opulent comforts and dual aspect views.
Love bites   Dine handsomely off family silver under ancestral portraits, in a room aglow with candlelight.
Love it up   Explore the Dingle peninsula and the Burren; shoot or take aim at archery; dolphin watch at Kilrush; play golf at Greg Norman's new Doonbeg course.
Who loves?   Knights and damsels who demand deluxe.

You'll love   Lording it here in knightly style.

The Mustard Seed at Echo Lodge

Ballingarry, Co. Limerick
T +353 (0) 69 68508
F +353 (0) 69 68511
E mustard@indigo.ie
W www.mustardseed.ie
Daniel Mullane

18 rooms
€180 to €300 per room per night
Dinner from €52

Closed two weeks Feb and Christmas

From Adare village: take the N21
Killarney road, then first left (R581)
for Ballingarry. The hotel is on the
Newcastlewest road.
✈ Shannon

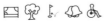

Things are pretty hot at the Mustard Seed – a top-notch restaurant set in a great hotel. The result is one of Ireland's biggest treats. Handsome and herbaceous-bordered, the sunshine-yellow former convent sits in seven flower-splashed acres on a hillside overlooking rustic Ballingarry. Owner Dan Mullane has restored the lovely grounds to provide synergy with the kitchen: that means perfectly ripened fruit, glossy veg and zinging herbs, plucked daily from orchard and kitchen garden. Menus respect ingredients and seasonality, and the award-showered cooking doesn't waver in quality. But if food's the thing, it's not the only thing. Expect style here without stuffiness. Individually designed bedrooms reflect the owner's travels and are snazzily appointed with a mix of antique furnishings, pleasing artworks and every modern comfort. There's a little fitness room to work off the calories, and a library stocked with good books to sink your head into. Come for dinner; come for dinner and sleep over; come for dinner and stay for a week. This place cuts the mustard.

Love time   Treat yourselves to a duplex suite for bags of space and unspoilt views.
Love bites   Cooking here hits the spot. Feast on tempura of oysters on horseradish mash, pan-fried sea bass with cauliflower and cumin puree, or pan-seared Irish sirloin steak with wild mushroom ravioli and pepper compote.
Love it up   Trawl through Adare's antique shops (it's said to be Ireland's best village), explore the Ring of Kerry and the Burren, or go walking and golfing.
Who loves?   Gourmets and gourmands, who else?

You'll love 🍃 Hot epicureanism. This place echoes with good living.

Moy House

Lahinch, Co. Clare
T +353 (0) 65 7082800
F +353 (0) 65 7082500
E moyhouse@eircom.net
W www.moyhouse.com
Bernie Merry

9 rooms
€200 to €239 per room per night
Dinner from €45

Closed Jan

From Shannon (one hour): take the N18 to Ennis and the N85 to Ennistimon and Lahinch. The hotel is a mile from Lahinch on the Milltown Malbay road.
✈ Shannon

There's a touch of *Wuthering Heights* about this white-walled 18th century country house set on a headland on County Clare's rugged coast – though we can't guarantee you'll see Heathcliffe striding through the door. More likely it will be twinkly manager Bernie Merry (who loves her guests to eat, drink and be merry), and whose hospitable staff offer the warmest of welcomes. Major restoration of this distinctive towered house in recent years ensures there's every modern comfort. Each of the nine oversized rooms is tastefully furnished, with dark wood furniture, warm colours and lashings of space. Many have generous canopied beds, with bathrooms beautifully tricked out in tile and chrome and fluffy robes as standard. Huge windows frame mesmerising ocean views. Watch the sun go down over Lahinch bay and the Cliffs of Moher while savouring a whiskey from the honesty bar. Then head upstairs to gaze out at the ever-changing moods of sky and sea. This is just the place to snuggle up tight on a stormy night.

Love time Themed in yellow and cobalt blue, Moy Mor has oodles of space, an original Victorian cast-iron bath and a shower the size of a dinner plate.

Love bites Chef Anna McGuane's cooking is a highlight. Menus change daily and major on imaginative use of local ingredients.

Love it up Lahinch is synonymous with golfing: you're in the St Andrews of Ireland. The new Greg Norman links at Doonbeg are close by, while clifftop walks, cycling and the glorious Burren coast await.

Who loves? Bon vivants who love their golf.

You'll love Watching mighty Atlantic rollers crash on the shore.

St Clerans

Craughwell, Co. Galway
T +353 (0) 91 846555
F +353 (0) 91 846752
E stclerans@iol.ie
W www.merv.com
Elizabeth O'Mahoney

12 rooms
€419 to €495 per room per night
Dinner from €65

Open all year

From Galway City: take the N6 East
for approx ten miles.
✈ Knock, Galway

When eminent film director John Huston left Hollywood, he settled here. No wonder; St Clerans is a picture. A handsome neo-classical building, it's set in 45 acres of scenic estate that includes the Dunkellin River and two waterfalls. Famed US talk-show host Merv Griffin later fell for St. Clerans and has since refurbished it handsomely. Guests can now enjoy this movie mogul's home frame by frame, pausing to zoom in on details like the splendid domed entrance, a grand drawing room complete with bold Chilean sunburst centrepiece on the ceiling, and a panelled library perfect for viewing beguiling Galway sunsets. Fires are lit in reception rooms, and staff are warming too. Spacious guest suites, a striking combo of trad and contemporary, more than honour their contracts (is yours pre-nuptial?) with expensive antiques and deepest thick-pile carpets. Blink, and you could imagine you're on a film set. Enjoy French and Japanese cuisine created with flair by French-trained Hisashi Kumagai, who also caters for weddings.

Love time They're grand rooms all, but consider an intimate close-up in the lovely Angelica suite, in the separate octagonal house.

Love bites Dine on the classics here alongside Japanese creations using seafood and organic produce.

Love it up Try riding and racing in Galway, hillwalking in Connemara, championship-course golfing in the area or hunting with the Galway Blazers. Pampering more your style? Book an in-room massage or beauty treatment.

Who loves? Real and Hollywood royalty, plus plenty of extras.

You'll love Feeling a tad star-struck.

Cashel House

Cashel, Connemara
Co. Galway
T +353 (0) 95 31001
F +353 (0) 95 31077
E res@cashel-house-hotel.com
W www.cashel-house-hotel.com
The McEvilly family

17 rooms, 13 suites
€170 to €250 per room per night
Dinner from €48

Closed early Jan – early Feb

From Galway City: Take the N59 to
Clifden. Turn left a mile west of
Recess on the R340.
✈ Knock, Galway

Connemara's rugged green landscape (and very green it is too) helps make Cashel House something of a west coast Irish idyll. Some 50 acres of secluded prize-winning gardens stocked with unusual shrubs and exotic Tibetan species envelop this peaceful 19th century building, lovingly run by owners the McEvillys. The place is pretty inside too, with Victorian and European antiques, heirlooms, flowers in profusion (perhaps magnolias, camellias and rare roses just plucked), and there's always a turf fire on the go. Bedrooms continue the gracious mood and throw in even more of those dreamy views, either of the bay or the splendid horticulture. This is one of Nature's gardens. Dermot and Kay's culinary skills make full use of fresh produce; there's freshly-caught fish in abundance, while carnivores get prime cuts and vegetarians never feel second best. Wash dinner down perhaps with a Château Lynch-Bages from the 100-strong wine list. The daily changing menu is served either in the picture-lined dining room or conservatory, with its picturesque views. Dreamy? Let's just say none of this is blarney.

Love time Some rooms offer views of the bay or Connemara's rolling hills. There's a cottage, too.

Love bites Five-course dinners feature freshly-caught fish, Connemara spring lamb or best Irish beef and gooey white chocolate cheesecake. Oh, go on!

Love it up There's a private sandy beach with swimming, while tennis, golf and mountain walks are close at hand.

Who loves? France's President de Gaulle loved to holiday here.

You'll love We think you'll be Cashel and... carried away!

Abbeyglen Castle

Sky Road, Clifden
Co. Galway
T +353 (0) 95 21201
F +353 (0) 95 21797
E info@abbeyglen.ie
W www.abbeyglen.ie
Paul Hughes

39 rooms
€198 to €262 per room per night
+ 12.5% service charge
Dinner included

Closed three weeks Jan

From Galway City: take the N59 to
Clifden. The hotel is situated half a
mile outside the town on the
Sky Road.
✈ Knock, Galway

Connemara has a way of inspiring its visitors to change the world, or at least making the earth move. Marconi transmitted the first commercial wireless message from Clifden in 1895 and, less than 25 years later, Alcock & Brown landed the first ever transatlantic flight here. Take the famous Sky road down from Clifden towards the sea and find Abbeyglen Castle, in 12 acres of sheltered parkland with waterfalls, streams, palms and a backdrop of the dramatic Twelve Bens mountains. Linger after dinner to sing a song around the Steinway piano, snuggle up on a cosy couch by the open turf fire or say goodnight to Gilbert the parrot as you climb the stairs to a vibrant bedroom tastefully decorated in classic style, with a canopied or four-poster bed and views across the bay. When hunter-gatherers go sea fishing, the chef is happy to prepare their catch for dinner in true gourmet style, whether it's a wrestled-for conger eel or blue shark, or simply a catch from the restaurant's aquarium.

Love time   Plenty of plump pillows and rich chintzes here. Get steamy in the spa's sauna or jacuzzi before beddy-byes.

Love bites   However you plan to work up an appetite, do it justice with locally caught salmon, shellfish and prize-winning Connemara lamb, expertly served.

Love it up   Take a Connemara safari – walking, picnicking or even island-hopping – through the region's wild and unspoilt terrain.

Who loves?   A favourite haunt of such legendary charmers as Peter O'Toole and Bill Clinton.

You'll love ❦   Great views across Clifden bay from those crenellated walls and turrets.

The Quay House

Beach Road, Clifden, Co. Galway
T +353 (0) 95 21369
F +353 (0) 95 21608
E thequay@iol.ie
W www.thequayhouse.com
Paddy & Julia Foyle

14 rooms
From €140 per room per night

Closed Nov – mid Mar

From Galway City: take the N59 to Clifden. The Quay House is eight minutes' walk from the town centre.
✈ Knock, Galway

Two centuries ago, the local harbourmaster built himself a magnificent waterfront townhouse in classic Georgian style. Now lovingly restored as a 14-bedroom guesthouse, it's an idyllic place to sit and dream of voyaging to distant lands as you watch the boats bobbing along the waterfront. Someone has obviously done just that, with oriental rugs, a draped tiger skin and elephant tusks propped in the hall, alongside the mounted fish and comfortable sofas looking out at the harbour. One visitor was inspired to describe the house as "a cross between a high-grade antique shop and the Natural History Museum." Floor-length windows, four-poster beds and turf fires are highlights in some of the calmly elegant bedrooms, while that over-the-horizon feel strikes again in the themed decor of the studios, from Napoleon to a safari special. All studios have private balconies.

Love time If the object of your desire is your own reflection, ask for the rooms with the mirrors behind the beds.

Love bites Breakfast is the only meal on offer, but the property is licensed, so relax with convivial after-dinner drinks, house party style. Snacks are always available and your hosts are happy to recommend local restaurants.

Love it up Escape into the rugged Connemara countryside, a perfect backdrop for hillwalking, horse riding, sailing, sea fishing or simply stretching out on the sand of some secluded bay.

Who loves? Hollywood aristocracy (Quentin Tarantino and Julia Ormond), some titled Europeans, and lots of honeymooners.

You'll love ♥ The big-hearted, off-the-wall welcome and an operatic eye for decor.

SCOTLAND – What's On

Och Aye... the year starts off with a bang North of the Border. If you miss all the fun and fireworks of a Scots Hogmanay, make time for Burn's Night festivities, some late summer Highland Games or the action-packed Edinburgh Festival.

JANUARY

Aviemore Dogsled Rally
Aviemore, Highlands
Watch more than 1,000 dogs straining at the leash on snow-covered slopes.
0845 225 5121 www.siberianhuskyclub.com

Burns Night – various venues
Scotland's national bard is celebrated on 25 January with a night of neeps, tatties and several wee drams.
www.visitscotland.com

FEBRUARY

Festival of Love
Glasgow
Scotland's second city celebrates its links to St Valentine with music, performance and film.
0141 204 4400

Inverness Music Festival
Inverness, Highlands
Now in its 82nd year, this festival attracts over 1,000 musical competitors.
01463 716 616

MARCH

StAnza Poetry Festival
St Andrews, Fife
World-class poetry in some atmospheric venues.
01334 472 021

Braemar Telemark Festival
Braemar, Aberdeenshire
Roll up with your snow gear for the UK's largest on- and off-piste ski party.
0845 225 5121

APRIL

Scottish Grand National
Ayr
The highlight of the Scottish horse racing year. Start placing your bets.
01292 264179

MAY

Speyside Whisky Festival
Various venues
A busy programme of events celebrating Scotland's whisky making heritage.
01343 542666 www.spiritofspeyside.com

Dundee Jazz Festival
Some of the hottest international names perform with the best of Scottish talent.
0131 553 4000

JUNE

UCI Mountain Bike World Cup
Fort William, Highlands
Thrills and spills are guaranteed in this world-class downhill and cross-country challenge
0131 557 3012

Royal Highland Show
Ingliston, nr. Edinburgh
Everyone's welcome at Scotland's annual farm, food and country spectacular.
0131 335 6236 www.rhass.org.uk

Royal Bank Glasgow Jazz Festival
Come for trad, blues and contemporary jazz.
01856 871445 www.summertimeinthecity.org

JULY

Open Golf Championship
Troon, Ayrshire
Watch the golfing heavyweights compete on the Royal Troon golf course (2005).
01334 460010 www.opengolf.com

AUGUST

Edinburgh International Festival
Most of August
This giant arts extravaganza makes Edinburgh a real festival city.
0131 473 2001 www.eif.co.uk

Highland Games
Piping, Highland dance, tossing the caber, tug-of-war and more at a variety of venues all summer. See local press for details.
www.visitscotland.com

Edinburgh Military Tattoo
A military spectacle of music, dance and pageantry at Edinburgh's historic castle.
08707 555 1188 www.edintattoo.co.uk

SEPTEMBER

Braemar Gathering
Spot the royals at this very Scottish games.
0845 225 5121 www.braemargathering.org

Doors Open
Venues across Scotland each weekend
A chance to see some of the country's hidden exteriors and architecture.
0141 221 1476 www.doorsopendays.org.uk

OCTOBER

Dunhill Links Championship
St Andrews, Fife
Watch the world's A-list golfers in action. Early rounds are also played at Carnoustie and Kingsbarns.
0870 010 9021

Glenfiddich Piping and Fiddling Championship
Blair Atholl, Perthshire
A major event in Scotland's traditional music calendar.
0845 225 5121

NOVEMBER

Glasgay!
Glasgow
The UK's largest multi-arts gay festival struts its stuff with music, comedy and club nights.
0141 334 7126 www.glasgay.co.uk

Glasgow On Ice
From late November
Lace up your blades on one of the largest outdoor ice rinks in Europe, with non-stop music.
0141 204 4400 www.glasgowguide.co.uk

DECEMBER

Capital Christmas
Edinburgh
A Christmas parade and open-air skating to mark the best of the season.
0845 225 5121
www.edinburghscapital.christmas.org

Edinburgh's Hogmanay
Where better to celebrate New Year?
Four event-packed days and nights.
0131 473 2056 www.edinburghshogmanay.org

FOR MORE INFORMATION:
0845 2255 121
www.visitscotland.com

ENGLAND – What's On

It's all happening here... the fun and fanfares of the season's top sporting events – whether horses, Henley or simply Hoorays – London's hot-ticket shows and festivals, and events galore country-wide.

JANUARY

New Year's Day Parade
London
Shake off your hangover and see the floats and bands leave Parliament Square at noon.
020 8566 8586 www.londonparade.co.uk

FEBRUARY

St Ives Feast and Hurling of the Silver Ball
St Ives, Cornwall
A silver ball is thrown into the waiting crowd and passed along beaches and streets.
01736 797840

Chinese New Year
Chinatown, London
Lion and dragon dance parades, plus fireworks in Leicester Square.
020 7851 6686 www.chinatown-online.co.uk

MARCH

Oxford and Cambridge Boat Race
River Thames, West London
This annual race between the two university sides starts at Putney and finishes at Mortlake.
www.theboatrace.org

APRIL

Cheltenham International Jazz Festival
Cheltenham
Chill to the sound of the sax with top names from Europe.
01242 227979 www.cheltenhamfestivals.co.uk

Chelsea Arts Fair
Chelsea Old Town Hall, London
The big collectors' fair: come here for brilliant paintings, drawings and sculpture.
www.penman-fairs.co.uk

MAY

Glorious Goodwood
Unmissable horse racing in the heart of Sussex.
01243 755030
www.goodwood.co.uk

Chelsea Flower Show
Royal Hospital Chelsea, London
Plants, flowers for all seasons, theme gardens and exotica.
0870 906 3781 www.rhs.org.uk

Badminton Horse Trials
Badminton, Gloucestershire
A stately home, the world's finest horses and the beautiful people - a three-day event.
0870 242 3436 www.badminton-horse.co.uk

JUNE

Aldeburgh Festival
Snape, Suffolk
Now one of the country's premier musical events.
01728 687110 www.aldeburgh.co.uk

Glastonbury Music Festival
Glastonbury, Somerset
Big names and small. Pack your bags and a bar of soap.
0871 220 0260 www.glastonburyfestivals.co.uk

Royal Ascot
York
With Ascot closed for redevelopment, the gala of racing, royals and hats moves North to York.
01344 876876 www.ascot.co.uk

Wimbledon Tennis Championships
Wimbledon, London
What a racket... the world's premier tennis tournament comes to town.
020 8971 2473 www.wimbledon.org

JULY

Henley Regatta
Henley-on-Thames, Oxfordshire
Straw boaters, hampers and oarsmen...
England at its colourful best. Take a hamper.
01491 572153 www.hrr.co.uk

The Proms
Mid-July to mid-Sept
Royal Albert Hall, London
Supremely British two-month long programme of popular concerts, opera and choral works.
020 7589 8212 www.bbc.co.uk/proms

AUGUST

Cowes Week
Cowes, Isle of Wight
Another summer season special – this time under sail on the Solent.
01983 295744
www.cowesweek3.co.uk

SEPTEMBER

Great British Cheese Festival
Blenheim Palace, Oxfordshire
A cheese lover's delight, all right.
0845 2412026 www.thecheeseweb.com

Burghley Horse Trials
Stamford, Lincs
Fabulous gathering of international three-day eventers in glorious English countryside.
01780 752131 www.burghley-horse.co.uk

OCTOBER

Ilkley Literature Festival
Ilkley, Yorkshire
The North's oldest literature festival, in one of the region's prettiest towns.
01943 816714 www.ilkleyliteraturefestival.co.uk

Newcastle Comedy Festival
Newcastle-upon-Tyne
Comedy festival with over 200 events and shows at venues in the Geordie capital.
0191 246 2565

NOVEMBER

Lord Mayor's Show
City of London
Watch the bands and floats parade through the City, before seeing fireworks over the Thames.
020 7606 3030 www.lordmayorsshow.org

London to Brighton
Veteran Car Run
See the cream of classic cars compete in this fun rally, starting at Hyde Park.
01753 681736 www.vccofgb.co.uk

DECEMBER

Christmas Lights – the big switch-on
Regent Street, London
Regent Street is closed for a star-studded concert leading up to a celebrity switch-on.
020 7440 5530

FOR MORE INFORMATION:
020 8846 9000
www.visitengland.com

WALES – What's On

Wales is a winner on the cultural front, with a language that's undergoing a vibrant rebirth. Don't miss a rugby international at Cardiff's showpiece Millennium stadium, the Welsh culture-and-carnival atmosphere of an Eisteddfod or summertime jazz at Brecon.

JANUARY

New Year's Day Dip
Saundersfoot, Pembrokeshire
Seems you can't keep the locals out of the water. They're a hardy lot.
01437 720 556 www.stdavidspenknifeclub.co.uk

New Year Celebrations
Cardiff Bay and city centre
Join in Cardiff's lively New Year celebrations, and rollerblade at an outdoor skating rink.
029 2022 7281 www.cardiff.gov.uk

FEBRUARY

Six Nations – Wales v. England
Millennium Stadium, Cardiff
One of a series of major rugby internationals held at Cardiff's showpiece stadium.
08705 582582 www.millenniumstadium.com

MARCH

St. David's Day
Throughout Wales
Costumes, daffodils, leeks and pageants celebrate Wales's patron saint on 1 March.
www.stdavidsdayfest.com

APRIL

Cleddau Waterway Festival
Pembrokeshire
April - October
Sea shanty evenings, exhibitions, storytelling, carnivals and son et lumières celebrate the Milford Haven waterway.
www.planed.org.uk

MAY

Hay Festival of Literature
Hay-on-Wye, Powys
Here's a chance to indulge your taste in books, food, comedy, music, gardens and literature in Wales's book capital. Scores of bookshops to browse through.
0870 990 1299 www.hayfestival.com

Swansea Bay Summer Festival
May - September
Swansea Bay gets in the carnival spirit, with Brazilian samba, beer drinking contests and outdoor theatre.
01792 635433 www.swanseabayfestival.net

JUNE

Wales Open
Celtic Manor Resort, Newport
See some of the world's top golfing names in action here.
01633 410318 www.walesopen.com

JULY

Royal Welsh Show
Builth Wells, Powys
This is the prime shop window for farming in Wales. Prize bulls, sheepdog trials, arts and crafts… it's all here.
01982 553683 www.rwas.co.uk

The Big Cheese
Caerphilly
An extravaganza of street entertainment, music, dance, fun fairs, folk dancing, falconry, fire eating, minstrels and more.
029 2088 0011 www.caerphilly.gov.uk/bigcheese

AUGUST

National Eisteddfod
Bangor (2005); Swansea (2006)
This celebration of Wales's musical tradition – Europe's biggest travelling festival – has something for everyone. Competitions in singing, reciting and dancing vie with a Welsh food festival, and you could pop for a week here. Welsh is spoken throughout.
029 2076 3777 www.eisteddfod.org.uk

That's Jazz!
Brecon
Jazz up your life at the brilliant Brecon Jazz Festival, where some of the world's jazz greats play in 90 foot-tapping concerts.
01874 611622 www.breconjazz.co.uk

World Bog Snorkelling Championship
Llanwrtyd Wells, Powys
A chance to get into a wetsuit and into the mud.
01591 610666
http://llanwrtyd-wells.powys.org.uk/bog

Llandrindod Wells Victorian Festival
Llandrindod Wells, Powys
Bring your parasol and smelling salts for this Victoriana extravaganza.
01597 823441 www.victorianfestival.co.uk

SEPTEMBER

Honey Fair
Conwy, North Wales
700-year-old street fair started by King Edward I. Over a ton of honey is sold, along with stalls selling plants, seeds, Welsh crafts and home produce.
01492 650851

Grocers, Gurus and Gourmets
Abergavenny, Monmouthshire
Browse through over 100 stalls from Wales and the Borders, selling everything from the perfect pork pie to choccies.
01873 851643
www.abergavennyfoodfestival.com

OCTOBER

Eerie Evenings
Oakwood Country Park, Pembrokeshire
Are you brave enough for a ride in the dark for Hallowe'en at Wales's largest theme park?
01834 861889 www.oakwood-leisure.com

NOVEMBER

Dylan Thomas Festival
Swansea, Glamorgan
Get your fill of the Welsh national bard, not far from his home in Laugharne.
01792 463980 www.dylanthomas.org

Cardiff Screen Festival
Enjoy the best in Welsh film-making talent, with screenings and film forums.
029 2033 3300 www.sgrin.co.uk

DECEMBER

Mari Llwyd Torchlit Walk
Llanwrtyd Wells, Powys
A New Year's Eve re-enactment of Mari Llwyd, an old Welsh tradition involving a horse's skull on a long pole, taken from house to house to welcome in the New Year. Take a hip flask.
01591 610666
www.llanwrtyd-wells.powys.org.uk

FOR MORE INFORMATION:
0870 121 1251
www.visitwales.com

IRELAND – What's On

Head to the Emerald Isle (easier than ever with all those low-cost flights) for the music, the golf and some of Europe's top race meetings. Dublin's the place for colourful St Patrick's Day celebrations, while there's plenty going on elsewhere.

JANUARY

Lord Mayor's New Year's Day Parade
Dublin
A rousing celebration with Irish marching bands.
+353 (0) 1 679 9144 www.bandfest.ie

Cork: European City of Culture 2005
Jan-Dec
Over 250 events planned throughout the year.
+353 (0) 21 455 2005 www.cork2005.ie

FEBRUARY

Irish Baroque Orchestra Spring Festival
Dublin
A feast of music played on period instruments.
+353 (0) 1 633 7283
www.christchurchbaroque.com

MARCH

St Patrick's Day
Dublin
This is the biggie. Join in the party and enjoy Ireland's number one celebration on 17 March. Music, street theatre, parades and more.
+353 (0) 1 676 3205 www.stpatricksday.ie

The Wexford Book Festival
Wexford
A four-day festival with readings, workshops and competitions.
+353 (0) 53 22226 www.wexfordbook.com

APRIL

Cork International Choral Festival
Founded in 1954, this four-day event in Cork's City Hall is still going strong.
+353 (0) 21 984 7277 www.corkchoral.ie

Fleadh by the Feale
Limerick
One of Ireland's major traditional music festivals, with concerts and open-air entertainment.
+353 (0) 68 31109 www.fleadhbythefeale.com

MAY

Boylesports Irish Guineas Festival
Kildare
Europe's top horses compete for glory in the Irish 1,000 and 2,000 Guineas and Tattersalls Gold Cup, in a great weekend on the turf.
+353 (0) 45 441 205 www.curragh.ie

Bantry Mussel Fair
Bantry, Co, Cork
Enjoy seafood banquets and fireworks at this three-day event marking the harvesting of Bantry Bay mussels.
+353 (0) 27 50360 www.bantrymusselfair.ie

JUNE

The Murphy's Cat Laughs Festival
Kilkenny
Need a laugh? Over 50 comedians from around the world perform in 12 venues over the June bank holiday weekend.
+353 (0) 56 776 3837 www.thecatlaughs.com

Budweiser Irish Derby
Kildare
Start studying the form. Ireland's top summer racing weekend culminates in the nail-biting Irish Derby.
+353 (0) 45 441 205 www.curragh.ie

JULY

County Wexford Strawberry Fair
Enniscorthy, Co. Wexford
Bands, art shows, workshops, circus, busking and fireworks – not to mention the crowning of the Strawberry Queen.
+353 (0) 54 37800 www.strawberryfestival.ie

Kanturk Wild Boar Festival
Kanturk, Co. Cork
A festival of the people, for the people, by the people. You won't be boared.
+353 (0) 29 50882 wildboarfestival@hotmail.com

AUGUST

Brendan Kennelly Summer Festival
Ballylongford, Co. Kerry
Come for the literature, music, Irish dance and workshops. One of the area's most popular summertime events.
+353 (0) 68 43557
www.brendankennellyfestival.com

Feakle International Traditional Music Festival
Co. Clare
Five days of music, song and traditional ceilidhs in the West of Ireland.
+353 (0) 61 924322
www.feaklefestival.ie

Fleadh Cheoil na Eireann
Clonmel, Co. Tipperary
Three days of traditional Irish music, with over 10,000 performers.
+353 (0) 1 280 0295 www.comhaltas.com

SEPTEMBER

Dublin Fringe Festival
A much-acclaimed platform for new writing and experimental performance art.
+353 (0) 1 679 2320 www.fringefest.com

Clarenbridge Oyster Festival
Clarenbridge, Co. Galway
A celebration of music and food to mark the start of the oyster season.
+353 (0) 91 796 766 www.clarenbridge.com

OCTOBER

B.A.F.F.L.E.
Loughrea, Co. Galway
Baffled? So are we – though this festival of poetry and craic has something for everyone.
www.baffle.ie

Banks of the Foyle Hallowe'en Carnival
Derry, Northern Ireland
Week-long celebration of ghouls, ghosties and things that go bump in the night...
028 71 376 545 www.derrycity.gov.uk

NOVEMBER

Darklight Film Festival
Dublin
A showcase for films, documentaries, music videos and animations utilising digital technology.
+353 (0) 1 670 9017
www.darklight-filmfestival.com

DECEMBER

Winter Solstice at Brú na Bóinne
New Grange, Co. Meath
Watch the dawn rays illuminate the secret inner chamber of this vast 5,000-year-old burial site. There's a ten-year waiting list for places!
+353 (0) 1 647 3000 info@meathtourism.ie

FOR MORE INFORMATION:

0800 039 7000
www.tourismireland.com www.entertainment.ie

R·R SPECIAL EXTRAS

The symbol shown above denotes hotels offering Room for Romance readers special extras during their stay. Many of these offers are exclusive to you, so be sure to tell your hosts you found them through Room for Romance when booking. Room upgrades are subject to availability on your day of arrival, so cannot be guaranteed.

Abbeyglen Castle	room upgrade (subject to availability)
Amberley Castle	complimentary copy of Amberley Castle's 900-year centenary book
Ardanaiseig	bottle of champagne on arrival
Austwick Traddock	bottle of champagne on arrival
The Beaufort	20% discount on standard room tariffs
The Bell at Skenfrith	glass of champagne before dinner on first night
Bindon Country House	bottle of champagne when taking a short break. Room upgrade (subject to availability)
Brownes Hotel & Restaurant	welcome drink on arrival. room upgrade (subject to availability)
Broxton Hall	10% discount on standard room tariffs
Burgh Island	a complimentary cocktail each
Carrig House	complimentary tea, coffee and home-made biscuits on arrival. Room upgrade (subject to availability). Special extras for honeymooners with advance notice
Cashel House	room upgrade (subject to availability)
Castle Leslie	room upgrade (subject to availability). Chocolates and bubbly for guests staying two nights with dinner on both days
Charlton House & Monty's Spa	10% discount on Spa treatments
Combe House Hotel & Restaurant	welcome glass of chilled petit Chablis
Congham Hall Country House	room upgrade (subject to availability)
Cotswold House	bottle of champagne or afternoon tea or a gift from Hermès
Cromlix House	room upgrade (subject to availabiliy). 10% discount on full B&B tariff
Darroch Learg	1/2 bottle of champagne on arrival
Dorset Square	room upgrade (subject to availability). Welcome drink and chocolates. One-day LA Fitness pass
Eastacott Barton	bottle of wine on arrival
Eastwell Manor	bottle of champagne and chocolates
Egerton Grey	1/2 bottle of champagne on arrival
Eilean Iarmain	room upgrade (subject to availability)
Emlagh House	room upgrade (subject to availability)
Esseborne Manor	room upgrade (subject to availability) or 10% discount on a deluxe room
Frogg Manor	bottle of house champagne
The George Hotel	room upgrade (subject to availability), glass of champagne
Glin Castle	room upgrade (subject to availability) and a complimentary gift
Gorman's Clifftop House	complimentary day's bike hire
Hell Bay	bottle of Jacquart champagne on arrival
Holbeck Ghyll	complimentary room service breakfast
Kilgraney House	bottle of house champagne with two-night, two-dinner weekend stay
Knockinaam Lodge	1/2 bottle of champagne on arrival
The Lake Country House	room upgrade (subject to availability)
Lake Vyrnwy	bottle of champagne
Langtry Manor	bottle of wine with dinner on first evening
The Leonard	room upgrade (subject to availability)
Lewtrenchard Manor	Devonshire cream tea on arrival

Linthwaite House	bottle of champagne with a two-night stay or longer
Longueville House	tea on arrival and glass of champagne each before dinner
Longueville Manor	room upgrade (subject to availability)
Lovelady Shield	bottle of champagne
Maison Talbooth	bottle of house wine and special breakfast for two (smoked salmon and scrambled eggs). Room upgrade (subject to availability)
Miller's Residence	signed copy of Miller's Antiques Guide
Minmore House	1/2 bottle of champagne
The Morrison	Up to 50% off the Luxury for Less package (€900 instead of €1,660 per night at time of going to press, including dinner and breakfast for two, a bottle of champagne and strawberries, and accommodation in a penthouse suite. Similar savings on a Gourmet Delight package. Room upgrade (subject to availability)
Mount Somerset	1/2 bottle of champagne
Moy House	bottle of champagne
The Noel Arms	1/2 bottle of champagne
Northcote Manor	1/2 bottle of champagne
The Old Rectory Country House	1/2 bottle of champagne
One Devonshire Gardens	bowl of strawberries and rose petals in room on arrival
The Peat Inn	welcome glass of champagne
Penmaenuchaf Hall	room upgrade (subject to availability)
The Pier At Harwich	room upgrade (subject to availability)
Pool House	glass of wine before dinner and late check-out
The Portobello	1/2 bottle of champagne
Priory Bay	glass of champagne on arrival
Rampsbeck Country House	1/2 bottle of champagne on arrival
Riber Hall	1/2 bottle of champagne. Room upgrade (subject to availability)
Roman Camp	bottle of wine with dinner on first night
Royal Mile Residence	bottle of champagne plus an additional gift
Rufflets Country House	gift basket with chocolates, miniature whisky and aromatherapy oil
Sheene Mill	glass of champagne
St Clerans	room upgrade (subject to availability)
St Tudno Hotel	bottle of wine in room
The Stafford	bottle of house champagne
Thornbury Castle	bottle of Thornbury Castle wine. Room upgrade (subject to availability)
Wallett's Court Country House	bottle of champagne on stays of two nights or more
Wineport Lodge	complimentray his-and-hers massage (30 mins) with every two-night stay
Wolfscastle Country Hotel	bottle of champagne

And now for the smallprint...

The offers detailed here – for instance room upgrades – are subject to availability at the time of arrival. While the hotels named here have elected to provide the extras and offers listed to individuals identifying themselves at the time of booking as Room for Romance readers, the publishers cannot accept responsibility for hotels failing to honour any offer. (This may happen if, for instance, a hotel's ownership changes and the new proprietors choose not to fulfil undertakings made by previous owners). Nor can the publishers assume responsibility for any loss, damage, disappointment, injury or inconvenience suffered as a result of a hotel's failure to honour any offer listed here. We recommend that readers confirm their booking, with details of the Room for Romance extras shown here, by email or letter.

WHAT'S YOUR TYPE?

Know the kind of place you're after but not sure where to find it? These listings should help point you in the right direction.

ROOM FOR ROMANCE – FRANCE

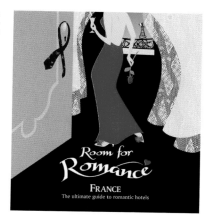

"... lists 120 of the country's most ravishing and seductive places to stay"
The Times

If this edition of Room for Romance has inspired you to take off on a romantic getaway, you need a copy of our sister edition Room for Romance – France. In short, it's the consummate guide for a Gallic getaway.

If you and your grand amour are looking for a sumptuous chateau in the Loire, a rustic Alpine hideaway, an intimate auberge in Provence or a chic townhouse on the Left Bank, look no further.

You'll find the crème de la crème of French hotels in this 164-page guide, with details of 120 ravishing places to stay in locations ranging from Picardy to the Pyrenees – with lots in between.

Hotels perfect for falling into temptation range from grand turreted chateaux to former troglodyte caves. Slumber in canopied splendour in a château seemingly straight out of a Proustian novel, bed down in an old Romany caravan, live like a prince and princess in the châtelain's own home, stay at a charming maison d'hôte that won't break the bank or check into the plushest of palaces for the ultimate in indulgence.

There are dreamy castles in the Dordogne, rustic Breton manors, Mediterranean villas and even a hip Camargue ranch. Some of the places featured boast sybaritic spas, others are on islands, while yet more have played host over the years to stars, kings and royal mistresses.

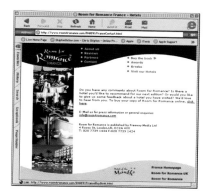

"Feeling frisky, passionate or head over heels in love?
Room for Romance – France checks out France's best beds"
Maision de la France Presse

You can buy a copy of Room for Romance – France online at
www.room4romance.com
or by calling 020 7739 1434. Copies cost £10.95.

INDEX BY HOTEL NAME

INDEX BY PLACE NAME

USEFUL CONTACTS

VISITOR INFORMATION

Visit Britain
020 8846 9000 www.visitbritain.com

Visit Scotland
0131 332 2433 www.visitscotland.com

Visit England
020 8846 9000 www.visitengland.com

Visit Wales
029 2049 9909 www.visitwales.com

London Tourist Board
020 7234 5800
www.londontouristboard.com

Jersey Tourism
01534 500 700 www.jersey.com

Ireland
+353 (0) 1 602 4000 (Dublin)
0800 039 7000 (UK) www.ireland.travel.ie

Dublin
+353 (0) 1 605 7700 www.visitdublin.com

Northern Ireland
028 9023 1221
www.discovernorthernireland.com

RAIL OPERATORS

National Rail Enquiries
0845 748 4950 www.nationalrail.co.uk

First Great Western
08457 484 950
www.greatwesterntrains.co.uk

GNER
08457 225 225 www.gner.co.uk

Midland Mainline
08457 484 950
www.midlandmainline.com

Scotrail
08457 550 033 www.scotrail.co.uk

South West Trains
08456 000 650
www.southwesttrains.co.uk

Virgin Trains
08457 222 333 www.virgin.com/trains

CAR HIRE

Alamo
0870 400 4562 www.alamo.co.uk

Avis
08700 100 287 www.avis.co.uk

Budget
0870 153 9170 www.budget.co.uk

EasyCar
0906 333 3333 www.easycar.com

Europcar
08705 996 699 www.europcar.co.uk

Hertz
0870 844 8844 www.hertz.co.uk

Holiday Autos
0870 400 4447
www.holidayautos.co.uk

National
0116 217 3884
www.nationalcar.co.uk

CLASSIC CARS

The Classic Car Collection
01923 775570
www.classic-carhire.com

Classic Car Hire
0845 230 8308
www.classic-car-hire.co.uk

Bespokes
020 7833 8000
www.bespokes.co.uk

AIR TRAVEL

The following airlines operate between the
UK and Ireland:

Ryanair
0871 246 0000 www.ryanair.com

BA
0870 850 9850 www.ba.com

EasyJet
0871 750 0100 www.easyjet.com

BMI
0870 607 0555 www.flybmi.com

Aer Lingus
0845 084 4444
www.aerlingus.com

Aer Arann
0800 587 2324 www.aerarann.ie